PRAISE FOR T\

"*Two@SJSU* is a gift, a contemporary anthology rich with life stories and fresh voices. These pieces strike quickly to the heart. They reveal with humor and poignancy the workings of very human minds."
—**Kate Evans**, author of *For the May Queen* and *Complementary Colors*

"The stories in the anthology, *TWO@SJSU*, offers a glimpse into the lives and imaginations of a talented group of writers—some of whom I had the pleasure of having in my classes. More than that, however, *TWO@SJSU* gives voice to a diverse set of writers who express the sometimes funny, sometimes poignant, sometimes crazy, moments of being human. I enjoyed reading these stories and seeing how students who begin with words and sentences weave together whole stories and whole universes. A delight to read and a pride for the SJSU community!"
— **Dr. Persis Karim**, author of *Tremors: New Fiction by Iranian American Writers, Does the Land Remember Me?: A Memoir of Palestine,* and *Let Me Tell You Where I've Been: New Writing by Women of the Iranian Diaspora*

"Caveat Lector: Flash non-fiction is addictive. A surprise-prize inside. Brevity is the soul of it. No one can read just one."
— **Dr. Scott Lankford**, Professor of English, Foothill College Center for a Sustainable Future, author of *Tahoe Beneath the Surface*

"A rich and rewarding anthology! I loved the variety of styles, viewpoints, and subject matters. There's a new treasure to be discovered on every page. Highly recommended!"

— **Scott Munson**, Playwright

"In a California park, the dog Friday races free; in Istanbul's Spice Market, a tourist finds an ancient toilet; at trailer park in Georgia, a romantic teen shudders with fear. Settings and moods shift in this energetic volume. Each two-pager is a glimpse of the lives we lead: a father who moves out and then away; a swimming lesson long delayed. Read this book to appreciate the narrative impulse—how important it is to track the ordinary and extraordinary moments of our lives."

— **Dr. Susan Shillinglaw**, Author of *Carol and John Steinbeck: Portrait of a Marriage* (University of Nevada P, 2013) and *On Reading The Grapes of Wrath* (Penguin, 2014)

"Short, incisive glimpses of life. Snapshots of moments that might not seem important at the time but are instructive and often life changing in the long run."

— **Bob Woodward**, career magazine journalist, writer, and editor

When Nick Flynn reads this book, he's going to say, "*TWO@SJSU* is the bomb!"

— **Nick Flynn**, author of *Some Ether, Blind Huber, Another Bullshit Night in Suck City, The Ticking is the Bomb,* and *The Reenactments*

TWO@SJSU

TWO@SJSU

An Anthology of Flash Nonfiction
From San José State University

Edited by Steve "Spike" Wong and Jan McCutcheon

Featuring original work by Adnan Adnan,
Jesse Buchanan, Valerie Cruz, Sage Curtis, Maria D'Avolio,
Shannon Daly, Ashley Florimonte, Kelly Harrison,
Jessica Keaton, Chris Krohn, Jon Linsao, Jan McCutcheon,
Deena Majeed, Jesse Mardian, Marcus Moonshoe,
Onette Morales, Amanda C. Morin,
Nahida S. Nisa, Alexander Papoulias, Tara Phillips,
Sarah Lyn Rogers, Marc Solkov, Amber Stucky,
Manni Valencia, Brett Vickers, Jennifer Voight,
Ria Vyas, Steve "Spike" Wong, Emily Wood,
and Candice Wynne

PUSHPEN PRESS | SAN JOSÉ CALIFORNIA

Library of Congress Cataloging-in-Publication Data is Available.
Paperback ISBN 978-0-9896676-0-9
E-reader ISBN 978-0-9896676-1-6

Printed in the United States of America 2013

EXECUTIVE EDITOR, ARTISTIC DIRECTOR, AND DECIDER IN CHIEF
Steve "Spike" Wong, stevespikewong@comcast.net

MANAGING EDITOR
Jan McCutcheon, jmccutcheon@gmail.com

SENIOR EDITOR
Kelly "Eagle Eye" Harrison

EDITOR
Tara Phillips

COPY EDITORS
Kulsoom Ahsan
Sage Curtis
Jessica Keaton
Sarah Lyn Rogers
Jennifer Voight

MARKETING
Sage Curtis
Steve "Spike" Wong

PHOTOGRAPHS, COVER DESIGN, PAGE LAYOUT
Jan McCutcheon

ARTWORK
Emily Wood

TWO@SJSU is dedicated to Professor Cathleen Miller who continuously inspires her flock to take flight.

CONTENTS

About TWO@SJSU

Steve "Spike" Wong and Jan McCutcheon

Steve "Spike" Wong grew up and still chills out in the state-of-being known as Santa Cruz, California. A high school English and Drama teacher for 38 years, he is on a mission: say it before you die. He has published work as varied as plays, academic work, ski writing, nonfiction short stories, and a small libretto or two. Speaking of two, he has that number of children, that number of marriages, that number of cameras, and that number of climbing boots. He has far more surfboards than necessary, and thinks of each session as a rebirth. He looks for the poetic in his writing, the powerful, purposeful and profane in his experiences, and love in every nook and cranny of life.

Jan McCutcheon grew up in Western Pennsylvania where she distinguished herself as a world-class truant. Making up for her aggressive lack of academic interest in high school, she went on to spend more time in community college than most students have been alive. Jan is currently working on a memoir that is a dark comedy about family, death, and the mafia. She lives in San José with her engineer husband, snarky teenage daughter, and very good dog.

TWO@SJSU. Spike came up with the idea for the project. He pitched the idea to Jan. They shook hands and decided to go for it. The goals of the project were to learn how to publish a book and to have an excuse to continue working with the group of friends fondly referred to as Cathy Miller's Flock. Various themes were posted on a Facebook page and writers submitted their works. This does not fully explain why so many of the stories submitted were about Batman. The editors and writers hope you enjoy reading these stories as much as they enjoyed creating them.

FOREWORD

Cathleen Miller

I looked around the classroom on that cold winter afternoon on the first day of the semester and registered an odd trend in the room…one I hadn't witnessed before. A handful of guys sat staring at me with an expression just shy of panic. True, it was my first time teaching this class, Intro to Creative Nonfiction, but I'd taught several writing courses at Penn State and never encountered this phenomenon before.

As Cathy talked the other people in my head held a secret meeting, conferring about what could possibly be the explanation for this invasion of terrified guys…and I noticed they were all guys. And they all seemed to be a certain type of guy because they all wore flannel shirts. Oh good, one of the voices said, we're onto something now. (During this confab the team of my other personalities was doing what they like to call, "creating a narrative to support events.") Yes, this tribe definitely had a fashion statement going on, they concluded, and it involved flannel with camo accessories. Hmmm. During a blackout had I posed as a centerfold for *Field and Stream*?

After class I took up the questionnaire I'd had them fill out and discovered the answer. The flannel-and-camo lads were all Forestry majors and for some inexplicable reason their curriculum required them to pass creative nonfiction. They knew much more about setting hooks than they did about setting scenes and their anxiety formed a cloud which I could feel hovering over us in the room. Each class they barraged me with questions croaked out in shaky voices.

Whoa, we have to do something to help the Forestry dudes so they don't fail the class, fill their waders with rocks and jump in the river. So I announced we would do a baby step before each assignment: we'd write a mini essay of only two pages, double spaced, and it would not be graded.

Thus began the two pagers.

An interesting thing happened when students cranked out diminutive non-graded papers: these assignments routinely became the best writing in the class. During twenty years of teaching I have introduced the 2P in every course, and even in my graduate seminars I noticed they offered an undeniable trend toward vivacity, freshness—and by virtue of the strictly enforced page limit—concision. The whole class would write on the same prompt, topics which varied from the soul of a place to 101 things I hate; yet I marveled at the wild variety of results, the avalanche of creative approaches.

Down through the years the two pagers have taken on a life of their own, finding homes in alternative weeklies, metro dailies, op-ed columns, literary journals, and even NPR. At least one 2P took steroids and ballooned into a memoir. And now Jan McCutcheon and Steve Wong, two of my remarkable former students, have given these flash essays their own anthology to provide the form with a unique showcase.

Oh, and the Forestry majors? By spring they'd conquered their fear and blossomed into talented nature writers, taking to the page like a duck to water.

INTRODUCTION

Steve "Spike" Wong

The Chinese philosopher known as Lao Tzu (although the actual existence of a single man with this rather honorific name is questionable) wrote something like, "Great acts are made up of small deeds."

TWO is a collection of small deeds by new writers (most of whom are young, but that is a relative observation and open to interpretation) at San José State University. Each story is non-fiction, and the writing is restricted to two pages.

Professor Cathleen Miller (who is indeed a friend of mine now that I have tried my best to get her to believe I am weird, feisty, and Zen, sometimes all at once) launched most of these authors into the exercise she calls "two-pagers."

Each two-pager comes complete with one instruction (although the opportunity to go way out-of-bounds is inherent in the simplest, seemingly most direct instructions): write two pages on _____ (fill in the blank with a topic, ranging from childhood to space to…).

For *TWO*, we handed out certain topics (like the "say what?" suggestion of "Batman"), but in general we accepted anything that conformed to the bottom line: two pages. Period (although a bunch of these authors stretched their definitions of two pages, but I can count and damn it you will make this fit two pages double-spaced or you are gone!).

Mark Twain (can we go without mentioning him? No. Ernest Hemingway believed all American literature came from one source: *Adventures of Huckleberry Finn*) said: "Get your facts first, then you can distort them as you please." And therein lies some of the danger and controversy in creative non-fiction.

As creative non-fiction writers, we have to earn the trust of our readers. (After all, there's a damn good reason why Nietzsche wrote, "I'm not upset that you lied to me. I'm upset that from now on I can't believe you.") That trust comes from…well, who the hell knows? I don't. I write. I creatively choose words and hope they contain enough truth to present an even greater one. (But let's not forget our earlier friend, Lao Tzu, who also said,

"The truth is not always beautiful, nor beautiful words the truth." So for all of our editors out there, don't get too pompous in your work, for the beautiful word is not always the truth. Especially if you're Chinese.)

The original idea was to include chapters that allowed certain themes to cluster together, to avoid a random and scattered collection of stories (although I have it from my childhood friend, Chris, a hunter, that a shotgun hits the target precisely because of its scattered shot pattern). It quickly became apparent that any sort of chapter-ization of the book would be entirely forced. Ergo: forget the chapters.

More than anything, we wanted these stories heard. We appreciated the opportunities to work with these talented writers and our die-hard staff. And more than anything, I owe Jan McCutcheon a big kiss and a huge hug for her focus, energy, determination and humor (although, when you think about it, writers and editors have to have some sort of unsettled commitment to an art that knows no end, and really, not even a period truly ends a thought. No matter what your English teacher told you).

Part One

How to Visit South Africa

Nahida S. Nisa

Mother, I am running away to South Africa. In the name of friendship.

These were words I never spoke to her. From many hours of childhood daydreaming, I knew how to go quietly, perhaps deceptively, with a single piece of carry-on luggage and about $200 folded into a passport cover. Bring a coat; it's winter there. Wear it on even the summery side of the world to save room—coats take up too much luggage space. Make sure everything you bring is beautiful. Forget to lock the carry-on as it is checked in. Ask yourself pseudo-philosophical questions ("Is it a carry-on if it's checked in?") and bury a hair iron into your handbag even though later one of the bride's friends will tell you your natural waves are gorgeous. Arrive in the middle of the night and descend upon a city so stunning that it looks as though God came home too tired to undress and laid down Her shimmering gold bracelets with sapphire accents.

Admire the bride's ring, also sapphire, diamond-haloed. Feel flattered that she will place it in the small jewelry box you've gifted her, the one engraved with the Sacred reminder that she is Endowed with "mutual rights." Tell her she is magnificent to compromise beliefs that are so integral to her soul for the sake of her family. At the ceremony, you will be impressed at how much she's managed anyway: half the men will stand at the balcony where you would have stood, had you not been attending the wedding of such a strong creature. Make eye contact and smile.

Behave as though you've always lived in Cape Town, and don't participate in any tours. See the city with your formally far-away friends and back away slowly from insistent baboons and inquisitive ostriches. Disapprove of the Township tours, but tell only them (your friends, of course, not the ostriches.) Learn that oarfish are the most fashionable of fishes. Drink lots of tea and the best lemonade you've ever had. Admire the museum artwork, a tall sculpture of a spectacular woman seizing the reins of a rearing horse as her navy and violet skirt streams behind its charge. *The Reign*.

It will rain, every day, including the day of the wedding, on which there will be a thunderstorm. Assure the distressed bride that this will make for fantastic photographs. Wear a simple slitted dress to the wedding for passive aggression, but don't cause trouble. (The blue of the skirt is too deep and too pretty of a tribute to her to be sacrificed for the fashion policing of oppressors.) Pray on the hills before lavender and turquoise shimmering lights under a silvery setting sun and realize again the prevailing Command of a supremely beautiful Divinity who could not care for the petty arguments of oppressive men. Remember the bride. Remember *The Reign*.

Lament only for the clouded sky masking the stars you never saw and will never see in your hemisphere. Halfway home to California, remove your coat.

TRY TO STOP ME, PANDORA

Sage Curtis

We should have kissed on the porch. In the rain. We should have gotten even closer than my arms wrapped around your waist; yours clamped uneasy on my shoulders. We couldn't leave the porch because of the rain.

Someone from the party could have walked out the front door. Then they'd see us, wrapped up together and we shouldn't be. Too much to drink, one more beer and I would have done it.

I saw it happening. You said, go inside, to your friend. Leaned in, got a little closer. Got a little braver.

We'd been at it all night anyway. It only took me a second to cross the kitchen and stand close enough. I touch everyone so you weren't special. You are special to someone, but she isn't here to stop me really. Tonight, I am special to everyone.

One more beer and I would have done it. Would have leaned in instead of away. Never would have said, no, I respect you and your girl, all while thinking, no I can't because I've got too much to lose.

Maybe it started in the backyard. At least, that's when the rain started. Under some cracks in the awning and my hair got a little wet. I said, no, to the cigarettes, I've got too much to lose.

Tell her no, said your friend, no one does it. Tell her no. And I'm just thinking, Douche bag, try to stop me. It makes it more fun anyway.

Maybe it all started on the beer pong table. I don't like to lose and all competitive, I'm yelling and you're watching me celebrate. Jumping up and down. I'm on fire tonight. One more beer to win.

We should have kissed on the porch in the rain, or left the porch for your car.

I was all cut-low Beatles t-shirt and tits. All purple tights and short shorts. And you were all tattoos and backwards hat. The rain was all wet and we were getting there, towards drenched anyway.

Maybe I would have done it with one more beer. Would have opened Pandora's Box.

Maybe then I would have gotten picked up, braced against the dirty wall, pushed against with hips and kissed like you might have kissed me. On the porch in the rain.

But I had too much to lose, it could have ruined me, made me into a liar because I know I would have lied.

And someone would have seen. Someone would know what we did then everyone would know what we did. I'd be the guilty one because I wanted it and no one stopped me. I'd be in trouble and you would probably have disappeared anyway.

Just one more beer and I might have done it. One more beer, or two, and I might have lain in your truck bed in the parking garage on the top floor, let your arm move from my shoulders to the small of my back.

We'd been at it all night anyway. We'd been at it for longer than that. We knew the possibilities of one more beer.

Someone said later: Ask me again if he'll ever try anything like that again, cause he won't.

Ask me again if I want you to, ask me again to let you kiss me on the porch in the rain. Ask me again to open up the box.

How was the party? I'm drenched in the rain. *Why were you outside?* We were hanging out on the porch, inside was a little warm. I'm going to sleep.

Ask me again and try to stop me.

Ain't What It Used To Be

Alexander Papoulias

She's running crazed with the football in the air. It's bigger than her head, but she's got her little teeth dug in and under the stitching, and now she's parading around in triumph. Tomorrow the football will be flat, but I don't care. I bought it for her—I just figured it would take her longer to destroy. It's a fall afternoon and we've got the field to ourselves.

I can let Friday off her leash when it's like this in the park. She'll listen to me and not run off if there aren't a lot of distractions. It's early, but the sun's already in my eyes and the silvery light makes long shadows of us on the field. It's warm and

15

bright, but the kids are in school and working folk are working, so Friday and I get to run. She will run and run and run herself to exhaustion and then lie there in the grass smiling and huffing and drooling. Her neck strains and her head reaches out to play some more even after her little body's run out of steam.

A group of girls from the college are cutting across the field, heading our way. Friday perks up and gives them all her attention. I do too.

"Oh my gawd! She's so sweet! What's her name?"

"Hi guys, this is Friday. Friday, say hello."

"Yarp yarp yarp!" she barks, right on cue.

"Ooooh, she's jus a wittou puppy! Can we pet her?"

"Of course. Long as you don't mind some doggie slobber. She's a lover." They crouch down close, petting and cooing and giggling. We get to talking. It's nice here. It's really nice.

A tug on the leash snaps me out of my memory. It's ten years in the future and I'm here again, in the park, now, today. Friday's stopped to squat and pee for the tenth time since we left the house. Her hind parts quake and shiver with arthritis when she lowers herself. It's not as easy now. Nothing is. She's got to have her walk, though. One block to the park, once around the field, and one block home. She wouldn't miss it.

"Oye, amigo," I hear, and turn around.

A soccer ball has rolled up to the two of us, and a young man is waiting on the periphery of his game for me to kick it back to him. I answer, "Yeah. Si—momento," and snap the ball with my instep. There is a small explosion in my knee, and I wonder if anyone else could hear the crack. *That was stupid.* Pain screams in my ruined joint, and I hop around trying to look casual as I regain my balance. *Nothing to see here. I'm fine. Just an old man walking his dog.* The ball rolls weakly before coming to a stop at what I guess to be the precise middle point between the young man and me. *Pinche daydreaming gringo.*

A group of girls from the college are cutting across the field, heading our way. I straighten up and suck in my gut, lean on the light pole to hide the gimp in my leg. *I bet they'll want to say Hi to Friday.* A sharp breeze picks up. It's getting cold and I forgot my hat. Friday's worn out. We should probably get back, so I give a tug and a whistle and we limp off. An old man and his old dog. The college girls only glance at us as we pass, and I wonder what they see.

WC

Tara Phillips

I had to go to the bathroom.

I wandered too long through rows of multi-colored spices in burlap sacks, squares of gooey Turkish delight in pistachio, coconut, or lemon, and thick Turkish coffee served in doll-sized, hand-painted cups. I avoided making eye contact with eight to ten black-haired Turkish salesmen offering "special good price" just for me on intricately woven wool carpets and blown-glass hanging lamps. Finally, I spotted a sign at the top of a concrete stairway that read "WC." After making my way down the steps, I paid a stout toothless Turkish woman one Lira (about seventy-five cents) for three tiny squares of one-ply tissue, and waited in a line of pushy women for one of the stalls to become vacant. As we stood shoulder to shoulder in the poorly ventilated and damp room, yet another stout Turkish woman used a large squeegee to mop the floor, pushing all the filthy water and garbage slush at a down-slope that headed toward the stalls. I laughed to myself at the foreign but charming absurdity of it. And now, whenever I think about the Istanbul spice market, I think about that bathroom.

After more than ten minutes and having one lady unapologetically cut in front of me, I finally got my turn in one of the stalls. The first three days of my Turkey trip, I'd been able to use regular, modern toilets, but not this time. Inside the tiny stall with a door that wouldn't stay all the way shut, there was a hole about the size of a basketball with two porcelain "step" spots on each side. Behind the hole was a tiny rusted floor faucet and a little red plastic bucket.

It was an old-fashioned, authentic Turkish toilet.

I could describe the work involved, including the required leg strength and the effort to lift any article of clothing that might get wet, and the necessity of a start-stop endeavor to avoid too much splashing, but I'll leave that part out and just point out one more thing: it turns out the bathroom's sole drainage system was the Turkish toilet holes themselves, so while I was in the stall, the cleaning lady pushed a wash of wet floor sludge at my feet just as she had done to the patrons before me. When I had finished and did what I could with my three small squares of tissue, I could barely open the metal door wide enough to get out of the stall because the next passenger was standing so eagerly close to it, awaiting her turn to get in.

While I can't say I enjoyed the experience of using the WC at the spice market in Istanbul, I walked back up the stairs with a smile on my face, knowing that it'd be one of those endearing, foreign things I'd remember about my trip to Turkey. I wandered back through all the colors and scents, pleasant and poor ones. I bought a bottle of water to pour over my contaminated shoes, met the tour group back at the bus, and shared with them an assortment of Turkish delight that I'd purchased at "special good price" from a salesman named Müjdat.

The Suit

Marcus Moonshoe

Sometimes at parties I do this trick called "The Batman." Listen—I am not proud about this. It isn't something I'd share with my parents. But sometimes when I've consumed the right amount of alcohol it seems like a good idea. The last time I preformed it was at a graduation party.

By the time I had arrived I was well off. My friend and I had been playing a game he liked to call "Heads or Tails." The game consists of spinning a coin and calling "heads" or "tails" and if you are wrong you take a shot. Yes, I know, great game. Anyways, probability had not been on my side, and I walked into the party feeling like a superhero.

Now, it is important to know that this wasn't a family-like graduation party, no; in fact I don't think there was anyone there over thirty. Everyone was like me—drifting along, as though in a trough between college life and the real world. Drinking games, drugs, and finding someone to fuck. How easy it is to avoid growing up. All you need is the right apathy.

After tapping the keg, I found the graduation girl and congratulated her on her diploma. She seemed relieved to be done. She told me of her bright future. Her internship. Her boyfriend's job. Moving to Portland. There was a picket fence in her future, a dog named Fido, probably a bunch of kids, vacations, retirement plans, death. But all I was doing was staring at her tits.

Sooner or later, I found myself upstairs in a room smoking pot with some friends. They were passing around a bong that was shaped like a toilet bowl. I remember feeling uneasy as I toked—as though I had done it too many times. And as I held the smoke in, I knew I was already gone. The release.

As we laughed about nothing, someone brought it up, someone mentioned "The Batman." After another toke and some egging on from the crowd of stoners, I acquiesced and headed down the stairs. In my mind, the Bat Suit was on—mask, armor, and all.

Listen—I am a disgusting pervert and I felt shame for weeks after this.

Followed by the stoners, I made my way around the party with my zipper down. I don't know why I chose to do it in the kitchen, but it was a populated area away from the music, so I probably thought it was the best place to get laughs. I found a stool and stood on it.

"Have you ever danced with the devil in the pale moonlight?" I yelled.

I pulled out my scrotum and spread the excess skin like batwings.

A friend would later tell me the details because I honestly don't remember what happened after. Maybe the excitement was too much. Anyways, he says that it wasn't received well. He says I was dragged out and thrown on the sidewalk by some jocks that didn't like the sight of another man's genitalia. He says some girl vomited afterwards, but I don't think that actually happened.

It will always be something to look back on. Remember when we were young? Remember when we could do anything? Remember, remember, remember?

But it is too recent now. Too real. Maybe it's time to move on. Forget who you once were. I graduate next May and after that? After all, there comes a time when a man must put one suit away and put on another.

EXPOSED

Amber Stucky

My pen has often poured poison as a prelude to the pain and this time is no different. I live in the margin, my life's story a quiet whisper amongst the bustle of community, a threadbare narrative strung along a deluge of anonymity. When I was young, whenever I was lost, I was found. Due to the life I was given, I will continue to search for my niche, my people, my tribe, my table in the corner, my cool kids bench in the quad. Due to my rage, I have mastered the art of being a raconteur, so everyone clap your hands together for this carnival of carnage!

She lives in a careful construct of lies, a fragile framework of family, a lingering and slow abandonment of her Self. She lives with a ripple effect of retaliation. She is a legendary lovelorn woman. I know her as an extravagant lush, a bitch I murder one poem at a time.

You have never been who I needed you to be. But I think we both know that.

I will expose you one piece at a time.

You have been boycotting me since the day I was born. You have hijacked my youth. You have a talent for tension, a man eater with a foul habit of mandatory manias, an oppressor who obsesses over obsolescence, an organizer of outrage, a parasite seeking pardon, a neglectful naysayer with negotiable love, a swagger with an evil syllabus exercising your surgical skill of suffocation.

Who could have foretold your fetish for flesh? Explain your game of senseless brutality and precious mockery.

My misery is the next part in the sequence of separation.

This dangerous delinquent has promised me defeat and she delivered. I have become more victimized than Jesus. I have stayed an angry simian maladjusted to the simple. I have become susceptible to suspense. I am left dehumanized. Just know, as you serenade me with your searing series of evil sermons that reconciliation requests are over. Keep grabbing because a gaudy garden of garbage is all you own.

I have settled into severance sweetly. Shameful serendipity this turned out to be: me living without you, you living without me.

Because of this premature assassination of my character, I have sharpened my wit and shaved my tolerance. Divide all that I have been and multiply that by what I wish I could be and there is nothing.

I am sorry that our lives ever entwined and that I ever sponged off you while I was setting up real estate inside you. I was nothing more than a placental pocket, fetal filth, a blockade to booze.

At the gates of Heaven I should be asking for a rebate, a blood refund.

I still suffer from the ultimate malapropism: mom. And still I pray to you, oh *perfect* palindrome.

Inside of you is a desire to be right for what you have done. Inside of me is a desire to be wrong for what I have not done.

OLD FLAME

Ashley Florimonte

The harsh sputter that jerks the cloud reigning over my lungs awakens every nerve in my body. Coughing has become an unwelcome ritual. I peer toward the flimsy curtain masking the overzealous morning, and groan. The wires in my brain come to life and I remember the night before. It is over. The monotonous duel that has ransacked my mind for seven years has finally come to an end. She is gone, and a melancholy fear aches in my bones.

Is this forever? I ask myself, as I become overwhelmed by the unwanted emptiness that rushes through my veins.

31

For seven years the romanticized persona of the relentless, pleasure-seeking, self-deprecating woman had overcome the intelligent and innocent being that innately occupied my psyche. For seven years, the two wrestled, tangling themselves in the wires that constituted mind and body, manipulating both to the point of exhaustion and emotional paralysis. Then there were changes, many changes, many positive changes, and I had decided that there must be a resolve—that the destruction of one persona did not necessarily result in a death, but did necessarily result in a compromise.

Thus the decision to quit smoking arose, and a most difficult decision it was. I was a writer, and the pen and keypad, in my mind, had always been intertwined with the soft abstract rhythm of nicotine and vapor rising from an unsteady hand. Kurt Vonnegut, Hunter S. Thompson, T. S. Eliot all yellowed their typewriters with tar dust and an unabashed calm that I romantically associated with the tobacco-human relationship.

I then realized that although I may have the potential to become as great as any of these writers, I was not required to habitually torture every system in my body (in order) to reserve a position in timelessness.

As I focus on the purity of air that inhabits every depth of my surroundings, she fights back. *It's 8:30*, she whispers.

My fists clench as I struggle to conquer the mundane habits that generate themselves in my fingertips, in the now vacant pocket of my tattered purse that I glance toward. "8:30" means nothing to me anymore, and I must remind myself the same of 9:30, 10:30, all the way to 4:30. "Morning coffee," "after dinner," "phone calls," "boredom," "a warm evening," "a rainy evening," and "nothing at all" are events that need remolding and appreciation as the concepts of time that flow into the rhythmic orchestra that is Day, rather than pieces that insist on cutting themselves off at every excuse and half-heartedly begin again until the next event calls for a break.

I inhale and exhale. 8:30 passes, and I am still alive. Why would I intentionally deprive myself of this gift that I have so fortuitously been given? Why would I fight to breathe when it is the one constant that keeps humanity leveled as one? My nerves regenerate, my mind calms, and her voice drifts away and is replaced by the ecstasy of a small freedom that I have permitted myself for the time being: life.

SEVENTY PERCENT OF LIFE

Steve "Spike" Wong

I'm on a red longboard floating on the steely blue. Seaweed gurgles to the surface like soft, brown jewels. Sunlight is just beginning to slice over the horizon, and for now the soft, rolling swells form the rhythm of life.

I think of Bob. Most of the time I do. I cup my hands, scoop some water, observe it and say to myself, "This is life." I wash the liquid cool over my face, and run my fingers languidly over my eyes, then cheeks, and finally my jaw, purposefully filling that moment with no other reason. And then I wonder why Bob had to kill himself.

35

When I found out the news, I wrote in my journal that Bob had things figured out, that growing old was not going to be a graceful process. He had planned things out completely for his family - money was never an issue with him - and then quietly ended his life. The powerful surge of his energy was gone, and this stood in stark contrast to even the flattest tide, which still teems with the weight and power of life on the calmest of days.

So Bob left.

...A steep wave approaches, and I yank my board around to paddle out to a better take-off spot. Every one in the water around me seems so at ease and so relaxed, but my excitement is tinted with fear. When I pick these waves, I start sliding and the next thing I know I'm heading straight for the bottom after falling backward, forward, sideways, and sometimes all three. It's precisely this out-of-control feeling that I imagine Bob must have felt, only it was significantly longer and more devastating for him. It must have been the sensation of getting sucked into an endless, bottomless close-out wave with an increasingly steeper face appearing below the pounding soup. Maytagged again and again, spit out onto the slick drop, out of control and tumbling, swept into more soup....over and over during his year of depression. A rag doll in Maverick's infamous break at fifty feet.

The picture lied. Two weeks before he killed himself by sitting in a small closet with a Hibachi loaded with glowing briquettes, Bob and I had a photo taken together. We were

36

smiling, which was usual, and wearing suits, which was not. We were at a high school homecoming football game. His son was the Homecoming King, and my daughter was the Homecoming Queen. It couldn't have been better. We were smiling, and two weeks later he was dead. From somewhere in the universe came the dark force that pulled the trigger in his head, the one accidental shift of his soul that a psychiatrist thought best would be adjusted with medication. It would prove to be the wrong idea.

Water is life. The protoplasm of the deep is our basic structure; it is the power that fuels us and, while living, makes us fear the unknown. When I get hammered eight or nine feet below the ocean's surface by a particularly strong wave and a characteristically bad take-off, I do fear never returning to the surface. I fear that blue will crash into black and all that is will cease to be. Yet maybe there is no more appropriate surrender to the inevitable than to return our seventy percent water to the ocean. Maybe it's the source of Bob's voice in my memories, this continuous cycle of wave energy that brings us happiness and fear as we await that last ride. Bob died alone, in a tiny closet lousy with carbon monoxide. If only life had called instead, we would be dancing on the water, joyful in our assumption that the last ride would be as celebrated as the first.

THE BATMAN

Brett Vickers

Would you like to go dancing with me?" he asks Sara, his eyes swimming down, past hers and beyond, resting somewhere below the collar of her shirt.

"No. We've been over this. I have a boyfriend and I don't dance." She doesn't make eye contact when she speaks. She's ignoring the gaze she feels lingering on her chest. Instead, she concentrates on the computer screen and punches in the appropriate produce codes.

"I could teach you how to dance," he says.

Sara shakes her head. She scans a box of cereal.

"Alright. How about a movie?"

"I have a boyfriend," she echoes, her voice stern now. All trace of professional courtesy has evaporated. She finalizes the transaction and waits for the receipt to print. She tries to hand it to him, but instead of grabbing the paper, he reaches for her fingers.

"Oh! You've got a manicure! How pretty! Your hands look... so soft."

She throws the receipt onto his lunging hands and turns to start the next order. He tries to get her attention again—to continue the one-sided conversation, but she only offers an apologetic smile. She's busy with another customer.

Sara and her coworkers call him Batman, but he's no suave Bruce Wayne, no athletic superhero, no caped crusader regulating the neighborhood's criminal activity. He's tall alright, but instead of being handsome, he is a pudgy degenerate. The thick, black rims of his glasses accentuate his pasty-white skin; his short, blonde hair provides no complement to his rugged complexion. He is perverted. He is dangerous.

He is a regular at Lunardi's Supermarket.

The employees call him Batman because they don't know his real name. In fact, they know very little about him. He pays for his groceries in cash and, due to the shirts he frequently wears and the questions of a curious bagger, they know that he works for Microsoft Game Studios in Sunnyvale. They know that he has a brat of a daughter who likes to scream loudly and run down the aisles, slamming the store's children's shopping cart into the shelves. They also know that his presence is something to be feared. And this Batman, just like the one in the comics, has a tendency to sneak up on people.

Once, he fondled the ribbon in Sara's hair while she was leaning over and grabbing an item from another customer's shopping cart. On multiple occasions he has complimented Jennifer, another employee, on her sexy, vibrant, red hair before requesting that she give his daughter a big hug. He is always asking the young female employees if they would like to hug his daughter.

The managers know about him, they know how he is around the female checkers; they know how he enjoys staring at the female baggers and asking them to help bring his groceries to his car as he follows closely behind. If the mangers see him, they come to the rescue, temporarily dismissing the women from their duties. The male courtesy clerks will take the place of the female courtesy clerks.

The women have learned to avoid him when he shops. They run to the back of the store and hide in the refrigerated milk box, hugging their bare arms in the cold room, soothing goose bumps and fears while peeking through the small window of the employee door. They wait for the call over the intercom, two beautiful words uttered softly by the manager on duty: *all clear*.

The women trudge back to their positions, masks of smiles pulled tight across their faces. Batman is gone for now, but he'll return. Meanwhile, there's work to do. There are other people to help. There are other customers to fear. Batman is just one of a cast of many twisted characters that demand interaction, that demand their attention.

This is retail.

Dialogue

Amanda C. Morin

J ust so I understand this correctly, Amanda, you are refusing
to take the breathalyzer?"

"Yes, I am."

"Please turn around and put your hands behind your back.
You are under arrest for driving over the legal limit of alcohol.

"We will get you down to the testing van so we can get your
blood results. You will then be transported to jail.

"Please follow me, watch your step as you go up the stairs.

"Hey Bill, how are you?"

"Oh you know, same shit, different day. Busy night? Amanda, I am going to need you to sit here, I will be removing one of your handcuffs.

"Aww, does that hurt? Little veins?"

"Yes, she does. I was going to use her hand but those are small too. Here, Amanda, you're done."

"Follow me Amanda. Watch your step, follow me to the truck. You will have to wait a few minutes before another officer comes to take you in."

"We are here. I need you to do exactly as I tell you. Step down from the van, walk through that sliding door and stand in the spot with the feet and wait for me."

"Good, now do you have any weapons the other officer did not confiscate from you?"

"Now walk through the metal detector and stop where the other mat with the feet is. Thank you, stay there until I tell you. We have another one."

"Miss Morin, I am a doctor here and I need to ask you some questions. Are you pregnant?"

"No."

"Do you have any medical conditions I should know about? High blood pressure?"

"No."

"Are you on any medication?"

"Zoloft."

"Do you know how many milligrams?"

"50 mg before bed."

"Alright, that is all. This officer here is going to take care of you."

"Miss Morin follow me, inside you go."

"What are you in for?"

"Apparently it's illegal to have two drinks. You?"

"I'm an idiot. I forgot my brass knuckles were in my bag and I tried to get through airport security with my kids. They told me to turn myself in and then it would be expunged from my record."

"Miss Morin? Follow me. Because you are on anti-depressants, we need to keep you out here for observation. I am going to handcuff you to this chair."

"Don't get near me, you honky trash. You're disgusting, throwing your wives that you beat up at home in here. And then you come 'n set me up. Disgusting pigs. Tried to rape my cunt!"

"Miss Reed, no one has done any such thing. Be quiet."

"I can smell your stank ass from here. Honky trash. Don't get behind me! Whatchyou doin back there? Don't you know who I am? Came here from another galaxy…got stuck in this place with you fuckin' honkies. They put that bag in my pant pocket and tried to rape my cunt. Nuh uh. Dis world's gonna end and all you honkies got your wives thrown in the slammer. Dissssssgusting!"

"Miss Morin, are you comfortable?"

THERAPY

Jan McCutcheon

My dog is the best walking companion. He's always willing to go and is a good listener if I have something I want to talk about. From the moment I drag myself out of bed and slide my feet into my fuzzy slippers and begin my trip to the coffee maker, he is at my side, leaping for joy. While the coffee brews, he paces back and forth between the cupboard and his dish. Half awake, I'm not paying enough attention to him, so he gently nudges the back of my leg until I fill his bowl. Lest I forget where his food is stored, he will go from bowl to cupboard until he is certain I'm on the right track because he knows I need some herding in the morning.

This morning, we rise an hour earlier than usual to go out into the wild world of Nature—in contrast to my usual destination into traffic. My dog wiggles in ecstasy as I attach his leash. He is unable to believe his great luck that we are going for a walk at this ungodly hour. The streets of my neighborhood are eerily quiet this Saturday morning. I'm hoping we will see the fat-assed raccoon that sometimes lurks near the "FLOWS TO CANOAS CREEK" storm drain, but today he is elsewhere. I'm hoping to see the snowy owl that sometimes flies above the elementary school, catching the light in a ghostly way, but we don't see him either. I am hoping we do not see the legendary neighborhood mountain lion.

We briskly walk the five residential blocks to the neighborhood park. Behind the park is a steep, bald hill. We climb up and up. I'm panting and slipping on the mud and wet grass. My dog is running ahead, pulling me as I huff my way along behind him. At the top, there is an uninterrupted 360-degree view of south San José and we're here for the morning show. Birds chirp, but I can't identify them. I'm sorry I didn't pay more attention to my parents and grandparents who could identify every birdcall, every plant, and every tree. Instead, I know the location of every coffee shop, bookstore, or restaurant in a twenty-mile radius. I realize that most of the Nature I experience these days is filtered through a car windshield with a soundtrack by NPR.

As we face east, in the direction of our house, the sky has a pale grey-orange glow. The dog sits at attention and faces east with me. Is he waiting for the sunrise or scanning for squirrels? More birds awaken. One is calling, "Caw, caw, caw, caw, caw!" Another answers, "Awk, awk, awk, awk, awk!" An airplane flies over low and loud, interrupting my mood, but the birds don't stop their cacophony. They have a lot to say in spite of the man-made interruption. The sky is gradually turning a lighter grey that is bordering on pale blue. Sunrise is taking longer than I expected and I'm cold. As the sky continues to lighten and unidentified birds shout their morning conversations, my dog and I scamper back down the hill towards home. We don't see the raccoon, the owl, or the mountain lion. My dog whimpers at the black and white cat slinking along the top of our fence. At daybreak, we are back in our kitchen and I make more coffee.

BARE BONES

Shannon Daly

At six in the morning, a thick layer of mist blankets the Feather River, yet untouched by roaring jet boats. Brett Brady is the first to arrive with his beloved boat trailing behind his 4-wheel-drive truck, aching to enter the Feather. The pleasantries are short. He greets me with a bear hug, and I get the feeling he may have a nervous breakdown if we don't get on the river, pronto. I climb quickly, albeit carefully into the jet boat, fully aware that I am now at the threshold of a man's heart and soul. Salmon is on the menu for today. The second we are launched into the river, the hunt begins.

51

Deep in the backwoods of North San Juan, California, Brett was born with a fishing rod in his hand. Still in diapers, he taught himself to fish using the bass pond behind his home with "a stick and a hook." Needless to say, his stick and hook days are well behind him, and he has moved on to bigger and better fish—literally. A licensed fishing guide operating in Northern California, Brett is widely respected—and feared—in the local fishing community. He can outwit any fish and outfish any guide.

When he's not on the river putting other guides to shame, Brett works for a public utility company—a job that pays the bills and puts food on the table. So why has he been guiding for over 13 years? Before I can get my answer, the rod to my right bends fiercely toward the water. I seize the rod only to realize I have no idea what to do with it. "Lift up, reel down, lift up, reel down," says Brett coolly as the salmon on the other end dives to the bottom of the river, stripping line faster than I can reel it in. About five minutes and two sore arms later, the fifteen-pound salmon slams into the boat and a smile the size of Texas stretches across Brett's sunburned face. I realize at this moment that he has answered my question: he simply loves to fish. "Find your passion, and do that," Brett frankly declares as he tosses my salmon in the cooler. Following my unexpected luck, Brett wastes no time baiting my hook—with salmon roe he cured himself—to get me back on the hunt. He flawlessly casts the line out into the olive-tinted water and shouts, "Do it again!"

Unlike the typical fishing guide drifting down the river, name splashed across the side of their flashy, accessorized boat, Brett is a minimalist. His nickname, "Bare Bones," speaks to his philosophy when it comes to fishing. His boat is sparse, containing only the necessities. He had the chairs specially mounted on a rail so they can slide easily out of the way when more room is needed for reeling in a monster fish. Even on a frigid fall morning, Brett wears only a camouflage jacket, sandals, and cargo shorts still stained pink from salmon roe on the last run—the mark of a good trip.

Most people equate fish in the boat with success. However, "It's not always about catching fish. It's the experience of being out here," Brett assures as he leans against the side of the boat, arms crossed casually in front of his chest, his wild eyes fixated on the spot where the line vanishes into the water. I gaze up and down the still river and appreciate the fact that Brett's boat is the only one for miles.

I now understand why he stays away from the crowds, even if it means staying away from an abundance of fish. "Sometimes you give up quantity for quality," affirms Brett. On this day, though, I haven't had to give up either. At high noon, with seven salmon in the cooler all weighing well over ten pounds, Brett has proven why he's the best.

101 Things I Hate

Jessica Keaton

I hate that people eat the organs of animals. That can't be sanitary. Think of all the gross things that go through those! I hate bones in meat. It just reminds me that I'm eating an animal and it makes me sad. I hate fishy tasting things. Maybe it's because when I was little, my daddy made me eat some of a lake bass. I puked it up and I don't think I've liked much seafood, other than Captain D's, since. I hate food that is surprisingly too spicy. When I'm expecting it, it's fine. But when I order a burrito and it burns my tongue off, I have an issue. I don't like to look at or touch uncooked meat. I think it goes back to the reason I hate bones.

I think I hate a lot of obvious things too—ignorance, homophobia, all of the -isms, dishonesty, hypocrisy, poverty, absolute power, Hitler, addiction, red tape, arbitrary rules, abuse, control-hungry people, societal constraints, bathing suit season, war, torture, women shaming other women, spiders, snakes, insects that sting or bite, violence, rudeness, asshole people, conflict, failure, fear, loneliness, change, feeling uncomfortable, brainwashing, traffic, people taking their anger out on others, people being late, creepy men, and smelly people on the bus. I think my reasons for hating these things are too blatant to cover and I'm sure other people hate them too.

Because I'm a converted California hippie liberal, there are some political things that I hate too. I hate those annoying political posts on Facebook. I almost hate it from both sides because I get tired of seeing it. I get it. I know how you feel. But I don't think it's really any of my business. So please. Don't. Also, I hate fundamentalists. Can I just say that I have an extreme hatred for the Westboro Baptist Church? And I totally think there's some weird, creepy sexual stuff going on in there. Since there is only one family who converted (idiots), there's got to be some major incest going on. Plus, I grew up in a similar environment, although the "Non-Denominationals" were more subtle about hating everyone. I hate corrupt politicians—on both sides—but

I really hate those homophobic Republicans who get caught in bathroom stalls with male hookers. Ugh. Once again, hypocrisy. I hate abstinence-only education because I think it really screws with people's heads (including mine). I just hate it when kids are brainwashed in general. It takes a monster to take advantage of people who don't know any better. I hate taxes on poor people. Why can't people who eat food that costs as much as my rent pay more taxes than me? I also hate it when people aren't friends with people once they find out their political views. I've had that happen and it's dumb and really hurts. I heard an episode of "This American Life" talking about how common this really is, and I think our polarizing media is to blame. But I won't go there.

I hate crappy books that get published while I get rejection letters—*Twilight, 50 Shades of Gray*, I'm talking to you. I hope you feel like you sold out for the rest of your life! I hate the Kardashians. They are famous for no reason. They have no talent or values and they are a bad influence on people who take reality television literally—like kids. I also hate skinny people clothing stores—nothing ever fits my hips, ass, or boobs in the really trendy stores that play blaring pop music with dim lighting and pictures of beautiful people on the walls. The clothing industry, along with the diet industry, can kiss my fat ass. I hate that I have bought into a certain amount of society's image of beauty and this kind of thing even affects my thinking. I hate that women are seen as objects and are still paid less than men. I hate how people think women are "sexually dysfunctional" because most men don't know female anatomy—this is because of a documentary I just watched on the pharmaceutical industry's search for female Viagra.

How to Wreck a Child's Confidence

Kelly A. Harrison

I didn't want to go to school even if my friend Brian was excited about it. His older brother was already in second grade and Brian wanted to do what his brother did. I was scared because the school was so big and I might get lost.

When my mom brought me on the first day, I clung to her leg as hard as I could. The kindergarten room was so big and full of colors and there were things on the windows that looked like the colored windows at church but they were made of paper and they glowed bright colors on the floor. My mom said I'd learn to make those and asked if I found that exciting, and I did, but not if it meant she wasn't going to be there with me. I wanted to learn how to do that at home, with my little sister and baby brother.

Some of the other mothers already left. Some kids were running around the tables. My mom took me to a corner of the room and showed me a place where I could put my coat. She called it a cubby hole and showed me how it already had my name on it. I don't know why, but I did not want to know about this. The jackets were in a dark part and I didn't want to go there.

She showed me the tables and how they were all small and had small chairs, but I was big, and the small chairs felt small to me but I knew some of the other kids probably liked them because they were little like the chairs, not tall like me. I was the tallest in my class, even taller than the boys.

My mom tricked me. She took me to the playground outside and said it was just for the kindergarteners. I saw large logs stacked for climbing, like Lincoln's house, and a swing set and she knew I loved swinging, but the best part was the tire. It swung on three chains and turned around and around. I could spin and spin and spin faster. Some kids didn't like spinning, but that was the funnest thing to do. The teacher came to the door and yelled for all of us to come in. Some kids listened and ran in, but she had to yell at me again and also Brian because he was sometimes on the tire and sometimes on the swing. That's when I learned my mom tricked me. When I went inside, she was gone.

The teacher wanted us all to sit on the floor to talk and she put us in order and we had a spot where we had to sit. I didn't like my spot because it was in the back. I wanted to sit in the front. I didn't want to listen in the back, so I started making up stuff in my head and she got mad because I was doing that when she got to me. I didn't know what I was supposed to say, so she had to tell me again and I got in trouble. Kindergarten wasn't much fun inside.

And then I found the best part of kindergarten was the bookshelf behind the teacher's desk. I found that on my own. No one was there. I sat in the corner reading a book. Someone's mom stood in front of me talking with the teacher. "Kelly, what are you doing," the teacher said when the mother moved to the side. "Reading a book," I said thinking it was clear what I was doing, but then she said to the mom, "How cute. She thinks she's reading!" After the mom left, my teacher asked me to read to her, so I did, but she thought I memorized the story and made me point to each word as I said it and then I got in trouble again. "Kids aren't supposed to know how to read in Kindergarten. Who taught you to read?" My mom did, I told the teacher, but I didn't want my mom to get in trouble, too.

Later, when I liked Kindergarten because of the play time and the paper projects and the giant jar of paste but not so much because of nap time, I had to leave class and go into a small room with this woman for testing. I had to read for her and plus and minus and things. We were in a small space with a lot of books and I didn't know her. I thought maybe I was in trouble again because of the reading even though she was nice about it. But I didn't like feeling bad, especially because I liked the stories so much.

THE WHOLE WORLD FOR A MOMENT OF PEACE

Manni Valencia

He lunges back and swings with all his weight. 240-pounds of All-American defensive linebacker (former) rushing through his arm and into his fist when suddenly his punch is caught, without so much as a grunt. A moment of shock as he takes a breath to evaluate what just occurred, but that short breath is interrupted by a bloodcurdling scream as his arm is twisted counter-clockwise. Pain erupts from his wrist and shoots through his forearm, past his upper arm and explodes in his shoulder. The pain is unreal, it's as though a thousand quills of molten lava are shooting out of his shoulder and arm. His vision is blurred from behind a veil of tears seeping uncontrollably from his eyes. They are hot and salty. He's on his knees now. He doesn't know when that happened. Snot dribbles down out of his nose and he's blabbering. Pleading for release. For forgiveness. For mercy.

He cranes his neck upward and masters his voice to utter one word, "Please."

Looming over him, the figure is clad in the night. His grip has no falter and his pulse is slower than the tides crashing against the docks in the distance. He smells of sweat and sulfur. The figure bends down impossibly low. It seems like he is taller than mountains and the act of lowering himself to that level takes just as long as it did to hue such a mountain. His stone expression from behind the cowl unbroken except from the gash made by his lips as they part to say...

"GET DOWN HERE! YOUR DINNER IS GETTING COLD!"

Sigh.

"Just a minute! I'm almost done with this chapter!"

I'm always getting called to dinner or to take out the trash or to help out with something, anything right when the best part is happening. I begrudgingly put down the comic. I trudge down the steps one by one. Left. Right. Left. Right. My hand dragging along the wooden bannister making a screech as my palm rubs up against the lamination on the wood.

Plopping down in my seat at the dinner table, most of the food is already eaten and cooling down. My older sister rushes off to get ready for some high school function that a measly 7th grader like myself wouldn't understand. My mother is feeding both of my baby sisters while my dad flips through channels on the nearby TV.

"Didn't you hear me calling you?" my dad asks, but it really sounds like a yell because that's how he talks. "What are you doing up there?"

"I was just reading some comics," I mumble as I heap food onto the plate in front of me. "You don't have to yell all the time."

"I'm not yelling. Besides, didn't I tell you not to read in your room. Those bulbs aren't good for your eyes. You should be reading under fluorescent lights like in the living room or kitchen. I keep telling you that you're going to go blind, but you don't listen. You never listen," my dad explains in a voice that no one would mistake for anything other than yelling.

"Sorry." It's all I ever say sometimes in my one-way conversations with my dad. The rest of dinner goes by without any more interaction between me and him. I excuse myself and race up the steps to my room. I nearly leap the distance from my door to my bed to find out what happens next.

"HEY, COME DOWN AND HELP WITH THE DISHES!"

Sigh.

LIKE CLOCKWORK, SCHOOLWORK

Brett Vickers

We find him still and quiet, very much like the muted night currently sagging against the glass of his bedroom window. Above the boy, slapped on the wall, grins a sly and bowler-hat-wearing Alex in all the two-dimensional glory that can be contained in a 24″ x 48″ poster. No other droogs in sight—which is the way Brett prefers these late nights. He is sitting comfortably in the chair at his desk, wearing… well, that's an interesting choice in wardrobe. Basketball shorts, baseball T-Shirt, scars from a mild scrap with an ugly stick, and woolly slippers: his usual lounging uniform. No one's going to see him at this hour, in this state of fashion disarray—not that he'd care if people *did* see him, but, still...I think that we can all partake in a collective sigh of relief that his look isn't of the trendsetting variety.

We're going to need a pair of X-ray goggles to see what he wears internally. Under the usual blankets of insecurity there are *quilts*—big, giant, Underground Railroad-style quilts signaling his inferiority complex—that are stitched with some heavy thread purchased from the Low Self-Esteem store (well, not purchased per se, he gets the material for free since he *owns* the store). Turn the knob on the goggles to amplify the vision. What do we see through this cage of hideous fabric but the skeleton of a rabid butterfly (not fluttering, mind you, but...) head-butting, *freaking dive bombing* Brett's heart whenever public speaking is part of the day's itinerary. The beast lies dormant for now, with one furry antenna propped up and listening for the cue, waiting for the slightest reason to attack with fury of a kamikaze squadron. One would think that a cocoon of blackness would render any creature unconscious, but it seems the absence of light serves as a conductor of paranoia. In the darkness, synapses in the brain fire away into infinity—fearing the connection to all that attempts to huddle alone.

Take the goggles off: the page remains blank, words beyond cognitive reach.

Hmm. Come to think of it, even Brett seems like he's asleep at the moment. He's been even more inactive than normal—not making much progress on… whatever it is that he is working on. It's hard to form an opinion on his endgame when there is just so much *nothing* going on at present.

Ah, there he goes to stand up and—wait. Nope. He's only adjusting lumbar support on the chair. No *real* movement goes on in this room beyond rhythmic tapping of foot against carpet, fingers skipping along keyboard and stomping upon mouse, the occasional flick and flourish of the right wrist to accelerate cursor across monitor. He's been still for the last half hour (yes, it really has been that long since that whole lumbar debacle) and there's no one around to check for a pulse. It's now two o'clock in the morning and it might be time to call the paramedics. No telling if he's breathing and there's an unnerving lack of moisture in the ol' corneasphere. Blood vessels are flowering, expanding into ocular orbit, reaching, stretching toward green iris with red talons unsheathed and engaging in some spectacle, some Christmas-y festival amongst arid canyons of the retina.

Blink.

Oh, gee, he's alive, folks. Rest easy now. There's life in this one yet. Not that we should particularly *care*, but, again, still… there certainly must be something happening in the boy's mind. And maybe—just maybe—one day he will find a way to articulate that which he means for us to hear.

69

APPLE-CORE

Chris Krohn

The Apple-Core, what's that?" Joey Pougiano asks, but in a way of not wanting to sound too uncool. With a five-foot tall father, and a mother who beats him with a wooden serving spoon in front of his friends, Joey Pudge is about as uncool a thirteen-year old, second-generation Long Island Italian kid you can be. He is forced to eat a lot too. Breakfast, lunch and dinner and a couple of coffee breaks he calls them, in-between. His Mother serves him steaming plates piled high with homemade manicotti, lasagna, and linguini topped with a clam and mussel red sauce as good as any restaurant in New York. This

71

plump, rotund kid can really eat when he's not running from his mom's large spoon.

"Pudge, let me see, how can I put it… the Apple Core's been around forever… like at least a coupla' weeks." He shakes his head and starts to cough. And when Pudge coughs anyone close is a target of what I call, the rain red. It's a washed-out red vomit. It sprays like water spewing out of a city fire hydrant sprinkler head on a hot day.

"Naw Kit" he tries to hold back a cough, "never heard of the Apple Core. Tell me something I don't know." Kit, that's me, named after Kit Carson the cowboy, and Kitty Carlisle the actress. Just then Pudge turns away from me and up comes a load of sauce.

"The Apple Core is just a bunch of guys hanging around the school yard, picking apples and throwing them at cars just for the chase." Between sauce heaves Pudge looks incredulous, like he's seeing the bearded lady, a la Ringling Brothers circus.

"Just guys getting together throwing apples for the hell of it?" He dissects his words. "Who chases you again?" Pudge's eyes bulge out, as he tries to stifle a cough.

"Well, the guy who gets his window busted out…or car dented, and by the cops.

"You're shittin' me." Pudge starts to laugh, and the hack is back. "Where do I sign up? Sounds like a real pissa." He is pleased, smiles and spits red again.

"Hey, yo! Calm down, don't start. Do not barf on me Pudge," I am firm, but jump out of the way just in case. He turns away and launches a big faded red gob.

"You're in business Joey P. We meet at three so, it's almost Apple Core's time!"

We walk steadily towards the Plaza schoolyard where the apple tree sits and where Pudge and me sat for seven long years before moving on to the Jr. High. Without warning there is a big thud, and then the sound of screeching tires. About a hundred feet away, in front of the school, we see several kids we know running. Shouts of "Holy shit!" are clearly audible. A wide-body bruiser with greasy hair in a white undershirt, a real live Hulk, is just closing his car trunk and begins moving toward us holding up a metal object.

"Looks like the Apple Core got started early today Pudge," I gulp air and we both begin to move at a quiet jog until we realize Hulk is headed toward us holding a tire iron.

"This way Pudge, this way." I whisper through my teeth in near panic.

"It's a dead end, are you kidding?" Pudge is already out of breath and gasping.

"I know this yard, just follow me." We escape over a fence covered in rose bush thorns. Both of us tear our arms on the bush and begin to bleed. Hulk is closing in.

"You fuckin' kids, I have you now." He lunges for us but gets caught in the bushes." Owww! I will catch you little shits!" Hulk is clearly not happy.

A police car pulls up. A single cherry top light is flashing. A cop steps out and looks toward Hulk. Pudge and I huddle on a nearby garage roof with eyes wide-open.

"But we didn't do anything. What'd we do?" Pudge whispers as I put my finger to my lips. The cop shines his flashlight our way. "I'm pissin, I'm pissin' in my pants." I roll quickly away to avoid the stream of urine now seeping out of Pudge's shorts. Steam appears as the warm piss touches the cold rooftop. Pudge laughs, "This is kinda fun."

BATMAN

Jennifer Voight

I'm Batman," he says, scrolling through his iPhone photos to show me a digitized polaroid of himself as a child, black masked, black caped, posing next to a faded blue Bigwheel, one proud foot perched on the plastic seat as if he'd hunted the thing down and subdued it himself.

"Ah yes, the superhero phase. Those were the days." I provide the obligatory grin, wondering how many people keep childhood pics of themselves on their phone. "And that's your Batwheel, yes?" But he's moved on, flipping through more photos while I help myself to the chips and dip, deciding there is nothing quite so stale as sitting across from someone at a restaurant while he massages his cellphone. So far I've made more eye contact with the waiter.

But Batman and I go way back. Though we haven't seen each other in about five years, we worked together for seven at a struggling software company across town, sharing a cubicle and a job we agreed was only big enough for one. We were friends. He reminds me of my brother, I of his sister. We even look alike: tall, dark hair, blue eyes, pale complexion, born in May and June of 1977, a thousand miles away from one another.

"Here it is!" A recent photo. Similar setup: black mask, black cape, but this time it's a car instead of a Bigwheel. A damn beautiful car. A shiny blue Mustang with its hood up, obviously at a car show. Batman is grinning wide in the photo, showing those big white teeth he's always been so proud of. Never needed braces, never had a cavity.

"Apparently the phase continues. These are the days," I laugh and inspect the photo, searching for other costumed car enthusiasts (maybe it's a Halloween themed car show?) in the background. Nothing.

"It's a long-standing joke with me and a couple of buddies," he says, finally excommunicating himself from the phone. It catnaps on the table near a bowl of guacamole.

"When I moved down to Santa Monica to partner in that restaurant. You remember? Yeah, anyway, there was this girl, Claudia, I think. She came in to the restaurant almost every night, and you know I'd just broken up with Anna. Anyway, the timing was really off, so I tried to just be cool with her, you know? Distant, just friends, but she....man she wouldn't give it up! So my buddy Chris, well, he brings in this mask and cape and I wear them all night and whenever she gets me alone I tell her, 'I'm Batman.'"

Batman's phone vibrates up against the bowl of guac and he glances down, presses a button, continues. "She finally gave it up after that, and ever since it's been an inside joke with me and my buddies. Whenever I'm in a situation like that....I'm Batman." I watch a glob of guacamole nosedive off his tortilla chip midway to his big white teeth and wonder what, exactly, he just told me.

"I'll be right back." I scoot out of the booth and head for the ladies room. Once there, I wash my hands and look in the mirror, inspecting dark hair, blue eyes, pale complexion. In photos I actually do look a lot like his sister.

I dry my hands, chuck the wad of paper towels at the garbage can across the room, open the door, straighten my spine, and head back toward our booth.

"Yeah, he's Batman alright."

I smile big at the waiter as he passes by with a tray of Coronas. A nice cold beer never looked so good.

One-Two-Vagina

Valerie Cruz

I added to the pile of small bits of paper as I strangled and tore at the napkin in my hand. I'm going to tell them I'm sick. I can have someone else say my part, but they might not get it right. We've worked so hard to put the Vagina Monologues up this year, Val, my friend who happens to share the same name, would kill me. "Okay everyone, we are going to start soon. I am going to do the introduction; it is time to be quiet." Most of the girls stopped talking while a few continued their conversation in whispers. With all the girls quiet, I was able to hear just how many people were there in the audience. It was a

Sunday, our last day. You would think that some of these people would have something better to do, and I swore when I came in, I recognized some of these people from the Friday showing. Why couldn't they go to an earlier showing, and why did my dad have to come? I was hoping he would have stayed home, but of course he wanted to see his little girl on stage.

I don't remember most of the play, only the parts where I said my lines. I had three sections. The first was just a reading of the type of clothing various women thought their vagina would wear. Not too bad. The second part was a serious portion, so that didn't really concern me either. What I was really worried about was the part I had next. I was still contemplating faking sick when Val introduced us.

"And now The Woman Who Liked to Make Vaginas Happy." I took a few breaths and followed the four other girls out onto the stage. Luckily I wasn't Jasmine, who was saying the full monologue. I would have messed it up for sure. Three other girls and I just had a few parts at the end. I tried to look at my dad once during the monologue after she was handed the horsewhip to see what his reaction was, but I could only look at him for a few seconds before I had to look away. I was way too nervous at this point, I really was going to be sick.

Okay relax, focus on all of the other people. Just pretend dad's not here.

Jasmine had finished her main part, and now she started listing off the various types of moans that there were.

Okay Valerie, just relax and say your part that you normally would.

"There is the Vaginal Clit moan"

"Mmmmmm, Ahhhhhh" I looked at my sister to see her reaction, I wasn't up to looking at my dad yet. She was laughing her head off. Either she thought it was really funny or she was laughing about how screwed I was. I couldn't tell which at the time.

"The Irish Catholic Moan".... Shit that's my line.

"Oh, OH FORGIVE ME...." I yelled out while throwing my hands over my head in prayer. I specifically chose this moan when we were picking out which moans we all wanted. I thought it was ironic considering I went to a private Catholic school when I was younger. Now, I wasn't so sure. Most of the audience members laughed so hard throughout our performance I thought they were going to slide out of their seats. We continued on with the moans, and by the time we got to the last one I was beyond caring. I was considering only doing the vocals and not the actions that went with this next one, but it couldn't get any worse, right?

"And now the Surprise Triple Orgasm moan."

That was when all of us on stage started "AHHH Ahhh" and pause "Ahhh Ahhh" pause again "Ahhhh Ahhhhh" and we all let lose. Trying to moan as loud as we could, some of us shaking, pretending to fall over, or actually falling over a little like I did. I was exhausted by this point when I looked over to where my dad was sitting.

"Hahaha." The entire audience was laughing, but I could hear him over everyone. At least he is laughing.

That's a good sign, right?

OF BOXES AND INBOXES

Onette Morales

The coffee pot was empty that morning. It was the last pot of coffee my parents would ever share. Well, that's what I speculated anyway. A shared pot of coffee had bonded the morning routines for nearly twenty years. It would be a shame if they didn't share at least one more on the morning of their final court date.

When I came back from class, my parents still hadn't come back home. The sunlight broke through the windows, staining our living room carpet, and highlighting the boxes housing my dad's

CDs and books. He had already moved his clothes and toiletries to the place I thought he'd be staying in.

I looked through one of the boxes. Inside were the scientific manuals and textbooks I'd always associated with my dad's job. When I was a young girl, I'd dreamed that one day I would be able to understand those books. I still couldn't. When my brother was a toddler, he chose one of the textbooks for his bedtime story. My dad laughed and went along with it, opening the book to a random page and reading a complicated explanation pertaining to a certain chemical compound. This memory, like many others that had resurfaced during those months, brought a familiar knot to my throat and the tears that followed. I had to get out of the house.

After three o'clock, I decided to walk back home. Back to reality—back to nostalgia. My brother would be home by this point. I needed to be at home to keep him from walking down memory lane alone. I unlocked the door and eyed the boxes that had prompted me to leave earlier. I rolled my eyes.

My brother came home before the boxes could tease me again. I put on my fake smile and got ready to repeat my new catchphrase ("It's all for the best") to any doubts or thoughts he might raise. We sat in the living room ready to turn on the television when we heard the top lock turn.

It was my father. He walked in with a half-smile. A charade he'd also adopted for my brother's sake. He carried a manila folder in one hand and his suit jacket in another. The brown suit jacket with the elbow pads my mom detested. I wondered if he'd worn that jacket to spite her. He placed the manila folder in one of his boxes.

"I'm going to put these in the car," he said.

When he came back in, he left the door open behind him.

"Okay guys, I'm going to go. I'll be staying at Arnold's house until I get my own place."

"When will we see you?"

"Soon. After I get settled in."

He hugged us and gave us each a kiss on the cheek.

"I didn't want this—you know I didn't. But I need you to remember that I will always love you both."

"I love you, Dad."

"Me too, I love you, Dad."

He walked out and closed the door behind him.

My father left nearly four years ago. He didn't tell us he was moving permanently; he left under the pretense that he'd be moving a few cities away. That was the plan. That was what we'd discussed. That was what we expected. Instead he ended up leaving the country. At least, that's what I've deduced based on the limited bits of information I've pieced together from our e-mails and his Facebook page.

Yet, every month I see his name, the name I used to see signing my field-trip permission slips and progress reports, pop up in my e-mail's inbox. My father, the man who taught me how to decipher chemical equations and enjoy the complexity of Pink Floyd albums, is now boiled down to a single message swimming among the sea of spam e-mails in my inbox. My father is now a combination of memories, words of advice, and song lyrics.

DRAT, NORA!

Maria D'Avolio

That Nora Ephron just ruined it all for me. There I was, perfectly happy, until I read her essay, "I feel bad about my neck." I hadn't gotten there yet, as I was too consumed with obsessing about the lines around my eyes, a luxury I should feel grateful for, not having to fight for my survival in a third world country. My Indian friend, Usha, would call this "problems on a full stomach."

Now I look in the mirror and my eyes go immediately to my neck, and I think of the mottled lumpy skin of a turkey. I have been moderately aware that my neck is not as smooth as it used to be. There is a little more loose flesh, and I notice when I look down, there are little skin rolls. In fact there is a double or triple chin that didn't used to be there. But I try not to look in the mirror when I'm looking down. That one time happened by accident when I was putting on lipstick in a make-up mirror and happened to be looking down, which I will never, ever do again.

For pictures my sister Connie swears by what she calls the half-swallow, where she swallows half-way and then stops. This tightens up her neck and makes it look more svelte. But my sister Terri and I take after Dad's side of the family. The half-swallow brings out the ropiness in our necks, adding another ten years, so it is in our best interest to take pictures looking upward towards the camera. Another of Connie's tricks.

When I was in my twenties and thirties, I swore that I was going to grow old gracefully. Now that I'm past that first blush, the thought of my face slowly taking on the shape and texture of one of those apple-head dolls, is becoming more of a reality. So is the thought of having a little work done. I do the same things that I used to laugh about when I read articles written by those older ladies who were having a tough time growing old gracefully. I pull back my hair to see what my forehead would look like wrinkle-free and the added bonus is that my eyes no longer sag. I think about what my friend, Kaye, told me after she had the new and improved face-lift so that her scars are on the top of her head.

"The pain is excruciating."

"Yes, Kaye, but would you make the same decision again?"

"Hell, yes!"

I used to say that the trade-off in wisdom was well worth it. "I wouldn't trade my wrinkles for the wisdom I've gained." Yes, spoken like a true thirty-eight year old who has not yet begun to see true decay. Yeah, pluck a few gray hairs here and there, drink more water, get extra sleep, and you look a little better. But pass that forty mark and it takes quite a bit more than that. And as Nora pointed out, aside from a major face-lift, there is not much one can do for the neck but cover it up.

But I have a feeling that Nora would be laughing at me right now, telling me to enjoy what I have, because in the not too distant future, I'll be looking back at this and wondering what I had to fuss about. "You should have counted your blessings honey. You didn't yet have to wear turtlenecks during the summer!"

BLACK NAIL POLISH

Deena Majeed

I closed my hand around the sparkly black nail polish and slipped it into my bag.

"Call Security," said the girl at the counter to her coworker; she turned toward me:

"Let me see your bag."

Oh crap. What did I do?

It was supposed to be an ordinary day. I was 16, and about to be arrested for petty theft. I was going through that rebellious time that many American teenage girls go through. Except I wasn't just American, I was Palestinian-American, born in

America with my roots set in Palestine located in Southwest Asia, or more commonly known as the Middle East. I was Muslim, and I practiced Islam. And stealing is not condoned in Islam.

"We're pressing charges," the worker said to me with a scowl on her face and her arms crossed.

"I didn't do it." Fight or Flight response. I went on defense and hoped that if I denied it enough the situation would go away.

Five minutes later, the police showed up.

"Put your hands behind your back."

I blinked. I thought this was maybe part of a prank TV show. The cameras would come out any moment. Then I felt the slap of the steel cuffs, the click of the lock, and the arm of the policeman escorting me to the police car. The friend I was with stood with her hands covering her face, mortified.

I have always been an honors student. In kindergarten I was fastidious about coloring within the lines, furiously balling up the paper and grabbing a fresh clean one if I made a mistake. I patiently waited until I was called on to speak. I did my chores before my mother had the chance to ask. So what was I doing at 16, getting arrested? And why couldn't I just ball up the paper and grab a new one and have a do-over? Because, I realized, this is what it means to be an adult, with adult consequences.

"Deena, are you okay?" My mother asked when she saw me. She thought they were wrong.

"Not my daughter!" I could imagine her shaking her head when they called her.

I went home ashamed, hurt, and terrified that I would be sent to prison for that damn nail polish. Looking back now, seven years later, it wasn't a big deal; I ended up having to do a week's worth of community service. For a sixteen-year-old girl though, every problem is the size of a colossal mountain. I needed to do something about it.

I went upstairs to my mother's bedroom, into her drawer, and I pulled out a lavender colored head scarf. I wrapped it around my hair, and I stepped outside. In Islam, women wear the hijab (head scarf) over their hair and cover their bodies as an act of modesty and worship to Allah (Arabic word for God).

I stole that nail polish because I felt confined within the boundaries of childhood. I wanted to break free, but I did it the wrong way. As I sat in my room that night, I thought back to my parents' homeland, and I thought of the religion that has enveloped me throughout my childhood, cradled me, taught me right from wrong. The moment I wore the hijab was the moment I choose my religion, the moment I grew up. Getting arrested was my wake-up call. I looked in the mirror with my hijab on. I felt beautiful.

WORD SEARCH

Marc Solkov

The train was full, or nearly full, backpacks consumed all empty seats. The train pulled to a stop. An elderly lady shuffled through the doors dragging a cart overflowing with paper, plastic, and survival. A plastic bag turned into a hood sheltered her hair. Her dress was faded and sandals too small. A man's windbreaker protected her shoulders. She looked up and down the train for an empty seat.

We met eyes.

I signaled her by moving my backpack and scooting in towards the window. She approached me, thanking me before sitting down. I welcomed her.

She twisted back and forth, burrowing a nest in her seat. Her elbow introduced itself to mine. She folded her hands in her lap and gently rocked from side to side. I sensed the weight of her loneliness suffocating our silence.

"Wutcha reading?" she said.

"A book for a class," I said.

"Is it any good?"

"It's not that great."

"I like to read, too." She pulled a thick novel out of her cart and handed it to me.

"Are romance novels your favorite?" I asked.

"Yeah, I like the gushy stuff, the sex and stuff," she chuckled.

"Me too."

She laughed and said I was funny.

I handed back her book.

"You're gonna have to take a test on that, huh?" she asked.

"Eventually, but not for a couple weeks."

We rode in silence for a couple stops while she excavated her cart. She dug up pages of old newspapers, empty water bottles, and half eaten chip bags. "Ah ha, found it." She held up a thin book of word search puzzles. She thumbed through the pages till she found a blank page. She stared at the puzzle.

"Hey, do you think I can borrow a pen?" she asked.

"Sure." I reached for my backpack. I pulled out the red, multi-ink, Mickey Mouse pen I had found on the train several weeks before. I handed it to her.

"Wow, this is cool." Her face lit up. She used her thumb to push down the different color tabs on the top of the pen, paying close attention to the way the colors interchanged.

She smiled as she circled words, alternating between the four colors with each discovery. She tilted her head towards my shoulder shrinking the gap between us.

I let her know my stop was next. She stood up and used her cart to balance herself as the train came to a stop.

"Here you go." She handed the pen to me as I stood up.

"No, keep it, it's yours."

She said nothing, just smiled, staring at me as if I saved her life.

"Best of luck on your test!" she yelled as I exited the train.

I looked back and thanked her with a wave, knowing that I'd do just fine.

CARDIO TAI CHI

Sarah Lyn Rogers

My final semester at State, I still need one PE unit. I sign up for Tai Chi, picturing elderly ladies I've seen out in Central Park working slowly through their sequences of smooth moves. If they can do it, I can.

My instructor—a small man clad in sweatpants and Chinese slippers—addresses the class with an affront to my expectations:

"You know those old people you always see doing Tai Chi out in the park?"

Yes, I think. *Teach me.*

"That's riding a bicycle. In this class, we will ride a motorcycle. Cardio Tai Chi is Tai Chi moves, but fast. I'll show you later this semester."

Pachelbel's *Canon in D* issues from my teacher's pink laptop. Meanwhile, he instructs us in training postures, which I understand to mean *aesthetically awkward and physically uncomfortable positions that will never look correct to him, not ever.*

For the duration of the semester, normal social boundaries are tested. Every class involves partnering with strangers and touching them in an attack so we can learn how to block (and be?) assailants. In real life, I am selective about skin contact and who gets to invade my personal space, but PE is an altered reality. I begin wearing jeans to class because I have seen too many wardrobe malfunctions involving see-through leggings during the training postures. If I'm going to show my hot young buttcheeks to someone, it will be on my terms, thank you.

After eight weeks of uncomfortable poses and a general sense of confusion, my class learns a sequence of movements that are taught to us as "Pizza, pizza, pizza, three baseballs, and then I tell you what next." My physical interpretation of these moves is about as graceful as they sound.

In a normal class setting, only the students who know the answers will make themselves visible. In PE world, all of the fumbling idiots are revealed, myself included. I spend every class period hoping that no one will look at me. All I want is to pass and graduate. I'm not good at the motions—I have arms, I guess? And I should move them?—but I feel guilty when someone shows me how to move better and I can't. Other people are invested in a version of my well-being which does not interest me.

For the final essay required for my one-unit PE class, I can choose between writing a five-page research paper with four sources, or attending a "spiritual event" related to Tai Chi. I picture meditation circles and sparks of energy and other nonthreatening New Age-y sounding stuff, and I agree to go to whatever it is. The flier for the event is written entirely in Kanji except for the address and time, so I shouldn't be so surprised when my boyfriend and I arrive at what is definitely a Chinese Christian church for worship service.

The next two hours feel like my class. We move our lips along to some God songs, sit and stand when we are told, shake hands with strangers, and finally watch as people literally fall over when the pastor touches them. I politely decline having my demons cast out or whatever is happening, then feel that I am disappointing others by not physically participating. I imagine everyone staring at me. When the pastor offers me a consolation blessing later, I take it. I am what I always was: worried about strangers making judgments about the way I move (or don't move) my body. Biding time. Posturing. Going through the motions.

ORIENTATION

Jesse Buchanan

L et's call it what it is: spoon-feeding commonsense to idiots. There is nothing of value within an orientation for someone who actually pays attention and follows the instructions given prior to orientation or in the emails that follow. Someone engaged in the material of success, the path, goals, and steps needed to obtain said success, have already read the material far before the people on stage stand and drone monotone at the crowd. Let us look to those members of society that need this material thrown at them repeatedly. See the dull look on their faces. See them fiddling about, texting, talking, drawing, and picking at themselves. Must those that know sit there waiting for the clock to pass the time in order for those that are disinterested in putting forth effort to be spoon fed the information again and again?

Here I sit pondering this again, my second orientation this week, this one being EOP, for financial aid in my studies. My thoughts return to the nightmare of the transfer orientation on Tuesday.

I arrived at the college fairly early, after all "The program will start promptly at 9:00AM; Students who arrive late will not be permitted to attend the event." I stand through the line to get my name-tag and then to collect my blue bag, pen, jump drive and folder. I arrive in the auditorium and I am guided like cattle to my seat, a small stiff-backed wooden monster that is hooked together in a row of around twelve. Beside my seat, well I say beside but the seats look as though they are made for children so truly half within my seat, there is a gal who is chit-chatting loudly with the gal beside her. Thankfully I am at the end of the row. I look up at the screen that slides between images that are supposed to keep me interested like some minor preview of the events I am to witness today. I see a calendar for testing come up, for the prior year. I can feel exactly how important the details are to the faculty. I realize that my iPod touch can tap into the wifi of the college and gingerly pass the time until the first presenter by checking my email and looking at my Facebook status. Yes, I

104

am killing time, until in walk a number of cheery looking teens wearing blue shirts.

The first presenter walks up and tries to bring about the crowd to attention and build up energy. But it is false energy, inauthentic yielding to her demands, nothing more. She drones on about deadlines. "There will be no exceptions," echoes over and over as I watch student after student walk into the auditorium late even though there was a warning of "students who arrive late with not be permitted to attend the event." My thoughts turn inward, "Yeah, you're serious." is all I can think. This continues for an hour at least. Then we are herded like cattle into the next stage of the event. All the while I am being threatened not to leave as there will be attendance all through the day and I will be expected to stay until the end, 3:30PM. I follow the rules, watching as professors and staff spoon feed commonsense to stubborn infants that lock their lips and keep looking away from the spoon. And those of us that follow instructions, that read directions, and understand the meaning of responsibility? We must suffer for those that can't.

Part Two

RECLAIMING FEMININITY

Nahida S. Nisa

Sometimes I think my aversion to small-talk is beginning to empty my life, as though there is a social reinforcer that I keep missing when I laugh politely, not knowing what's airy enough to say and wanting to ask something like, "Do you ever feel like sunlight on glass?" and cringe inwardly at the bizarre looks. When I say *I miss you* it means there is a graveyard and bats and a violin, and each string is an empty voice asking empty questions like nice weather isn't it? Is that a new hairstyle?

It isn't new sometimes I just wear it because there are perplexities orbiting my hair, planetary systems of paradoxes. These high heel stilettos are funeral shoes because I love them but it's been too many centuries and I've forgotten if I love them or if I only love them because you love them, kind of like believing red is my favorite color and then years later reading that you're attracted to red and wondering in paranoia if I've been conditioned, like touching jellyfish. When you ask me aren't I a radfem I am bitterly thinking I'm whatever you've made me to be, Pygmalion, as I blink away tears and you say, I guess the basis of that answer means you are—so what's with the mascara?

I say with love-struck anguish, it keeps me from seeing beautiful transparent rainbow molecules between my lashes. And you scowl. I wish you wouldn't do that to yourself.

I didn't.

Yesterday there was a tree at my window knocking to be let in. I traced over the architecture of my bones and took the laundry out and taught myself to fix the car and I read the books you love as a woman walked by the window with her skirt flowing behind her like a trail of broken verbs in the past tense. And I wished I had told you that mascara is like standing on a hill looking down at city lights with the oxygen escaping you and you're realizing that they are masking the beauty of the stars they imitate—the ones that inspire them—but you're unable to stop yourself from admiring this—

—artificial beauty. It's like that, you know? Being only human. I just want to be part of the universe. But I'm terrible at smalltalk so I tried to tell you about the documentary I saw instead, because it's not so strange when I say it isn't mine.

God, is anything real?

You can't reclaim femininity because you've never defined it, said the radfems, the patriarchy did. Scissors hung from a doorknob, days powdery like the powder you apply to your face. I say, it's gunpowder. They say, how do you know that soft black coat is feminine, womanly? Well I don't care because I move my nails beneath the thread that is coming undone at the seams just a little bit, coming undone like me. To what standard do you strive, but that set by men to say that masculinity is the ideal to which all women should aspire? Let women define what it is to be a lady, strength and fearlessness and love. Let us be who we are, manly women and womanly women and womanly men and manly men. This is to remind us whatever is feminine is of equal worth, not to be abandoned. Say the word orgasm and smile crookedly when it reminds you of rooms in July.

Satirists and the patriarchy scoff and say, nowadays everything is female empowerment. And I want to scream, *And does that tell you nothing?*

Lunchtimes

Adnan Adnan

Often, our lunches were stolen by the older kids. Big boys from the eighth to tenth grades behaved as if it was their right to steal younger boys' lunches. Because the big boys were required to pray during the lunchtime, they were allowed to go and pick up their lunches from the headmaster's office first. While they picked up theirs, they also grabbed as many packets as they could that belonged to the younger kids. At least twice a week, I would find out that mine was stolen. I wondered why the headmaster couldn't organize the picking-up better to prevent the stealing. We used to say, "Maybe the headmaster steals some, too, and that way he could blame it on the older boys. That's why he has a faulty system in place." In reality, stealing from the younger boys was a school tradition.

Our lunchtime was seventy-five minutes long. It gave us enough time to eat, pray, and play. Our Arabic teacher required that we all prayed during the lunchtime. He was a good old man, a big man with fat cheeks and a very long beard. He understood that we were boys. He was the only teacher who allowed the boys to settle their disputes by having a fistfight after school. We loved him for that. He also told us, "Pray as quickly as you can, and then go chase the girls from the girls' school." We loved him for that, too. Because he permitted it, we prayed at the speed of light, reducing the twenty minutes praying time to less than two.

After praying, we played a game called Thieves vs. Police, where we divided the group in two: one group pretended to be the thieves, and the other the police. The thieves were given five minutes to run away, and then the police would find and catch them. It was fun to be the thieves, because if you were caught last, then you were considered to be a great thief. It was the greatest honor one could earn playing that game. We played for about fifty minutes, and then we all showed up in front of the girls' school, and bothered as many girls as we could before heading back. I had to be careful there, since my mom had graduated from that same girls' school, and she still had a lot of her teachers there who often complained to her about me.

Usually, when I went home in the afternoons, my mom would say, "You went there again. I know it. I told you not to go there." I said things like, "That's a lie. I stopped going there a long time ago. Who complained? You shouldn't listen to just one of them. Did they all see me?" She would say, "This is really shameful for me. My teachers are always complaining about you." I would protest, "Maybe they mixed up the days. I didn't go there recently. I'm telling you the truth." I had to deny everything, and deny quickly, because I didn't want to be beaten by my mom.

My mom was notorious for beating me. My dad beat me only once in his life, and he was ashamed of it after, and still is. But my mom took great pride in beating. Sometimes people gathered in our house to see the show. Other mothers in the neighborhood would scare their boys by saying, "If you are not behaving like a good boy should, I will give you to Adnan's mother and she will kill you." It was a good working-system to control the bad boys. My mom would start by saying, "If I'm my father's daughter, I will teach you the biggest lesson of your life. You will never make this mistake again." She had an immense thirst for setting examples and breaking her own record, but I got used to it, and it didn't really hurt much after a while. Everyone within a mile and a half radius from our house knew about my mother's ruthlessness, and how she often beat me. But she never beat me for bothering the girls during my lunchtime. It is perhaps because my dad, when he was at my age, used to go to that same girls' school and bother

115

my mom. She probably couldn't beat me for the same things that they used to do during their lunchtimes.

In the Dark

Jennifer Voight

From that first miraculous trot across the open plain by Australopithecus a few million years ago, to Thomas Edison's bright idea in 1879, before incandescent bulbs, LED key-chains, iPhone flashlight apps and glowbars, it was damn dark at night on this planet. We developed lanterns of course, and had fire nearly from the get-go, but neither of these is especially portable from the best mode of transportation we had yet to devise: the back of a horse, so travel at night was a dark business no matter how you squinted at it. The most widely available light source for nocturnal equine travel has always been divine light. The moon. But here's a little-extrapolated fact: if you happen to be traveling through a mature forest at night? So much for divine light. It's as dark as a squid's wazoo at the bottom of the sea, full moon be damned. Up until around a century ago this was common knowledge, and when it was occasionally necessary to journey by horseback at night it's doubtful anyone told stories about the experience, unless of course some additional event in the dark made the ride tale-worthy.

Today, about 3 million people ride horses in America each year, with around 67 thousand of those intrepid equestrians being seriously injured. Of those 3 million, only a tiny percentage have ever ridden a horse in the dark, through open country, for any serious distance. First off, riding a horse—even in daylight—is not easy, and no instructor can teach the most crucial element involved. Balance: either you have it or you don't, and it's what keeps the horse between your butt and the ground.

To get a better understanding of equestrian balance, imagine straddling a wine barrel. Comfortable up there? Of course not. Now, imagine your wine barrel has approximately half a ton of muscle and bone, stands about eight feet tall, can bolt at nearly 40 miles per hour, produce almost 3,000 pounds per square inch (psi) of torque with each footfall, has a brain the size of a nectarine, and is programmed by evolution to panic in the face of danger. Now, with all that, imagine you're blind. Day or night, balance is what saves you from going soil sampling, no matter what anyone tells you.

Riding a horse in the dark produces a combination of controlled terror, exhilaration, and assuming things go well, the kind of trust reserved for the person who packs your parachute pre-skydive. If you don't trust your horse to try and keep you both safe, you're probably in trouble. And if you've failed to cognitively embrace the fact that what you're doing is statistically far more dangerous than skydiving, you're a lunatic.

Here's the amazing thing: horses can see at night. They have the largest eyes of any land mammal, and they have something called tapetum lucidum, (it's what reflects back at you in the dark when you shine a light at nocturnal creatures) which means they have superior night vision, and a smart horse—yes, some are smarter than others, trust me on this—will never intentionally hurt itself. So, as long as you stay topside, you're golden, sort of.

Approximately 90 percent of people riding in the dark for the first time lose their lunch along the way. It's understandable really; you're ten feet off an undulating ground you can't see, you have no sense of speed, nor can you see the apparatus (your trusty wine barrel) which propels you through space. You can't see the ditch or the hill or the tree or the puddle or the log or the imagined bogeyman your horse is avoiding; they're all the same woozy swerve left right up and down to you. And don't forget that it's late at night and your mind is playing tricks on you by now; a tired, frightened, and imaginative mind can do some truly amazing things. Add to that a steep technical trail in which your horse must negotiate rocks creek crossings tight turns narrow trails steep drop offs, and you can kiss your dinner good night.

When you arrive at your destination, the weakest of light will pain your fully dilated eyes and cause your stomach to compress itself to the size of your appendix, and the odds are good that you'd fail a sobriety test even if your favorite grandma's life depended on that linear line-dance. Stumbling, mumbling, squinting, and swerving, you will hand off your reins to the nearest human and dive straight for anything resembling a bed. Once there, the sensation of not moving elicits wonder and pure joy. In the morning, you hug that horse and cry your sincere gratitude into his mane, because you're alive to regret the hell-ride only because he kept you that way, in the dark.

A Whistle and a Bucket of Sand

Candice Wynne

When I checked into my room at the Lake Sandoval Lodge in the Peruvian rainforest, I found a piece of paper taped to the wall and on it was a brief and neatly typed message: "In case of emergency, this room is equipped with a whistle and a bucket of sand." No further instructions or even a hint of an explanation.

How curious. In all my world travels, I've never encountered a notice quite like this. I felt as if someone was passing on a secret code, a mystery for all jungle visitors to decipher. The whistle, hanging on a piece of string from a nail on the wall, I'm fairly sure, was to blow on if, perchance, one might find an intruder in one's lodging. Maybe a wandering crocodile, a slithering snake, or even a crazed revolutionary? Would it be more risky, I wondered, to put my mouth on the same whistle that someone with any number of contagious diseases may have also left their hideous spittle? or face the unwanted intruder myself? I suppose that would depend on the intruder.

And the bucket of sand—I'm just guessing here—wasn't meant for cigarette butts. Since the whole place was made of wood, bamboo, and dried palm fronds, accidentally setting the whole place on fire (and destroying the lodge in very short order) was a very real concern. I've never had to put a fire out with a bucket of sand, but I'm pretty sure it would barely cover a bed with mosquito netting. Anyone who is foolish enough to smoke in a bed with mosquito netting should just—stay home.

The third possible scenario would be a combination of the two: the room catches fire, and said occupant should either first grab the whistle and blow like hell and then grab the bucket of sand to smother the flames, or use the sand first and then the whistle. Bucket, whistle. Whistle, bucket. Luckily, I never had to make such a grave decision.

There are only a handful of lodges in the remote Tambopata Reserve along the Peru/Bolivian border. As always, I began planning months ahead and found that the location and programs offered at two or three jungle lodges coincided with my mental image of this once-in-a-lifetime adventure. Knowing this would probably be my only chance to experience this part of the world, I wanted to choose the right place for my needs: a remote basic lodge with an eco-educational theme. As it happened, Sandoval Lake Lodge was at the bottom of my list, but since I made the mistake of waiting several weeks for my travel companions to make up their minds, the more desirable lodges were completely booked by the time I received a decisive response. Note to self: make reservations first, then inform the rest of the party. Better for them to cancel than for me to forego a much preferred destination. Dismissing the fact that all our meals were prepared using the San Quentin Prison cookbook (circa 1960s), the lodge itself was acceptable.

I knew ahead of time just what to expect: this was the jungle, after all, and the primitive digs were part of the whole experience. The en suite bathrooms, though minimal, were quite a luxury (hot water was available only a few hours in the morning and again in the evening). Two long wings stretched from a large central hall, each with about twelve rooms with eight-foot walls and then open space up to the rafters. An elevated wooden plank porch ran the length of each building with chairs here and there for guests to enjoy a bit of reverie. The brown painted doors had sturdy locks; however, right next to each door was a window with nothing but screen and a roll-up shade, so anyone who really wanted to could simply reach through the screen, unlock the door and help themselves to a veritable cornucopia of bug spray, flashlights, granola bars, sun hats and bottles of pharmaceuticals. There were no thefts, at least not while I was there. Any would-be thief must have spotted the voodoo doll I made out of one of my socks and set in the center of the room—a granola bar in one hand and a pocket knife through its heart, eyes popping out of its head, tongue hanging to one side—a figure of exacting vengeance. Call it foolish, even primitive, but this was the jungle and I knew just how to protect myself.

A Conversation With Myself

Jon Linsao

Consider this: Your brain contains one-hundred billion neurons (that's billion with a *b*). Those neurons carry electrical impulses through your body, regulating your nervous system, your organs, your glands—every bodily function you possess. Our most staunch supercomputers are eons away from matching the sheer computational prowess of the human brain. So when I sit on the couch watching Joel Shumacher's *Batman & Robin* and wonder why Batman has rubber nipples on his Batsuit, I recognize that maybe, just maybe, my brain's true potential is wasted on me. And once I acknowledge this fact, I dive headlong into the topic of nipples in a conversation with myself.

Why *does* Batman have rubber nipples on his Batsuit? What purpose do the nipples serve? Do they detach, allowing Batman to throw them like Batarangs or throwing stars? How much damage could Batman possibly inflict with *throwing nipples*? The only conclusion to draw is that they're purely aesthetic. But isn't that a waste of rubber?

Well, yes. Rubber nipples are a waste of rubber (and a questionable financial investment), but if anyone could afford to purchase a lifetime supply of nipples, it would be Bruce Wayne. In fact, I would actively encourage Bruce Wayne to buy his nipples in bulk. Doing so would create monumental demand, rubber manufacturers would be forced to increase production to keep pace, and the rubber nipple industry would flourish (something the economy of Gotham City sorely needs). But where would Bruce Wayne keep that many nipples? I imagine Bruce Wayne might find a Batcave full of nipples distracting so he can't keep them in *there*. And he doesn't have enough Batsuits to attach the surplus nipples to, so what is Bruce Wayne to do?

Well, how does a Batsuit made entirely of spare nipples sound? Terrifying? I agree. What about a non-lethal firearm that takes nipples as ammunition, something akin to the rubber bullets that police use for riot control? A rubber nipple wound isn't fatal, but it is highly embarrassing. Consider the following scenario:

Two bank robbers meet back at a nondescript safe house after their bank heist is foiled by the Caped Crusader.

"Holy shit," says the first bank robber, peeling back his ski mask. "That was close. Hey Sonny, where'd all those tiny bruises come from?"

"Batman shot me in the face with that goddamn nipple gun of his," Sonny responds. "Tony, I don't think I wanna be a criminal no more if it means Batman'll shoot his nipples at me again."

I pause for a moment and look over what I've written. A piece of me wonders if publishing this story is a good idea; I mean, I just spent two hours writing and revising a story about Batman's nipples. *Batman's nipples.* How will that look to other people who read this story? And what will they think of me? But the initial hesitation is quickly quashed when I realize: I've found a use for rubber nipples. I'm an engineering genius. My brain's potential isn't being wasted. And swept up in a moment of hubris, I compose an email, attach this story, and hit send, hoping that there are others who will appreciate Batman's nipples like I do.

WHERE, OH WHERE...

Maria D'Avolio

I've gone and done it again. My journal has gone missing for about the third time in as many months, and I'm now ready to admit that someone as absent-minded as I am has no business whatsoever keeping one. In fact it's just plain irresponsible.

For those who may not keep one, the implications may not at first be obvious. After all, what does one write in a journal anyway? The dull, dry happenings of the day? A few thoughts about the meaning of life? Or the quirky goings-on of a mind run amok, along with thoughts that perhaps are better left unwritten? The latter would be me.

I have a horrible penchant for indiscriminately jotting down every thought that pops into my head, disregarding the warning bells of self-preservation. This potential powder keg could ignite if it fell into the wrong hands, and the wrong set of eyes alit upon a specific entry. It's only now that it's missing that I question why, oh why, didn't I evaluate any of my musings before putting pen to paper? And really, why don't I keep better track of the things I write?

As I traced every step I had taken during the last few days, trying to remember where I could have left it, some of the words I'd so carelessly written assaulted me and I began to feel a little sick. My journal definitely does not show me at my best. It constitutes a black and white record of all those naughty and irreverent thoughts that have ever come across my consciousness. I'm aware that many of them are thoughts that everyone has at one time or another, but when allowed to dissipate, the mind can then go to work on the white-washing and erasing that inevitably happens when we examine our own character, and we can continue to think we are really nice people. Write it down, and that is no longer an option. There is proof otherwise.

Aside from that, what would be the repercussions of someone finding it before I do?

Well, let's start with the possibilities if I left it at work. How does this entry sound?

"That witch of a boss is supposed to audit all the expense reports I process, and yet they sit on her desk day in and day out. Then a month or two later, when she finally deigns to review them, she dumps them on my desk with a hundred sticky notes attached with all her comments and action items. I swear if I see one more of those stickies I'm going to attach it to her face!"

Yep, that would get me big points if someone at work found this. Maybe I'd even get fired! Please don't let me have left this on my desk, in my rush to leave the office!

How about the home front, then, the contents of which I will not divulge, except to say that my children would think me incredibly hypocritical for telling them not to swear or say nasty things about people, while reading what I'd written about their dear daddy in one of my rages following a post-split spat.

And friendships? Well I'm sure I'd be quite popular with my neighbor if my children happened upon the one about her. It could potentially mean quite the narrowing of our social circle. I can just hear their sweet little voices when they're over at her house visiting,

"Mrs. Hazel, my mom doesn't think it looks very classy to write reminder notes all up and down your arms. How come you don't just use a pad of paper?"

The least troublesome area would be school, as I'm only taking one class, although my grade could possibly be affected.

"I couldn't believe my professor last week! She said some of the most..."

Uh oh. I really need to find that journal.

LIVING PAGES

Jessica Keaton

I always carried a book with me on days when we would travel across Georgia from Ellijay in the Northeast to Carrollton in the Central West. The drive was two and a half hours on curled backroads and I wanted to be anywhere but in the leather backseat of the Suburban. Rides were desperate and unspoken; the only voices letting us know we existed among other humans were the conservative voices on the AM radio.

I tried to tune them out—entering worlds that I could only dream about: ritzy New York, salty-aired California, and dreary Chicago. Usually, I was reading a book from the *Left Behind* series, taking comfort in God's control over the universe but I had finished all of the ones that were published. I was around thirteen or fourteen, which meant I had finished *The Remnant* and was waiting for *Armageddon* to be released. Instead, I switched to my other favorite author, Mary Higgins Clark. I had just watched the movie *Loves Music, Loves to Dance*, so I was eager to read the book. Despite the lack of a light source due to the shady windows and the curvy roads making my stomach swerve inside my skin, I didn't put the book down until I felt the Suburban slow and heard my father's voice.

"Get down in the floorboard," he said, eyes on the road. He turned the steering wheel and we were on a backroad somewhere in between Villa Rica and Temple, both suburbs of Carrollton.

"Why? Where are we?" The tone of his voice, along with my already heightened state of anxiety due to the book, made me panic.

"Just do as I say and get your ass down! This is no place for girls."

I panicked more, recalling *Loves Music*. In the book, the main character, Darcy Scott, goes in search of the man who killed her best friend, Erin Kelley. I was within pages of finishing it, watching the killer force Darcy to dance with him in his secluded house—just as he had danced with Erin before he killed her. I had just gotten to the part where Darcy had discovered a ring she had made Erin under the couch. Clearly, that was no place for girls either.

"But—"

"Do you *want* to get raped?"

His words astounded me and sent my brain into a tizzy.

Where is he taking me?

The Suburban stopped and my father, in his leather, Nascar jacket and Dollar Store aviators, opened the door.

"I'm serious," he lowered his tone, "stay down."

He slammed the door shut and, for a few minutes, I heeded his direction. But my curiosity got the best of me. If I was in danger, I wanted to know where I was in case I had to tell the cops later.

I thought I had seen every trailer park in Carroll County, but this was one that I'd never been to before. It was much more dingy than the one we used to live in. Old tires filled with rainwater lined yards. Plywood and tricycles dotted front porches and silver, diamond-shaped gates ran along the yard next to the gray trailer next to the Suburban.

This must be the one he went into—

Suddenly, a large, bald man wearing a wife beater walked in front of the Suburban. I tried to hide behind a seat, but he caught my gaze before I had a chance. His eyes didn't look scary or dangerous—mostly sad and zombie-like. He stared at me for a few minutes before he walked in the opposite direction.

Maybe Daddy was exaggerating—

The sound of a door opening caused me to drop to the floorboard again. Slowly, I rose again to see my father standing on the porch of the gray trailer reaching toward a hand inside. It was so dark that it looked like it wasn't attached to anything—like Thing in *The Addams Family*.

I remembered the *Loves Music* movie and how the killer was always shrouded in darkness until his identity was revealed at the end and hoped that hand in the doorway stayed cloaked in shadows. Holding my breath, I sank to the floorboard until I heard the sound of the door opening.

I have to stop reading all of these mystery books.

WATER

Amanda C. Morin

I spend my childhood along the coast of Soquel, where blue and yellow and white houses crown the undulating mounds of cliff. The white house on the corner of 18th Avenue is where nuns retreat for reflection and crucifixes hang above our sleeping heads. There is a small gravel alcove with white wooden chairs, weathered and flakey, reposing behind a low wood railing. Purple flowers with their crunchy leaves gushing with tacky sap cling to the edge of the cliff and tip-toe to the edge, unsure of taking the plunge.

The spicy scent of the juniper arch that surrounds the cliff wars with the tang of sea. Beyond is an infinite view of the grey sea—the icy Pacific. Every morning the fog rolls in and immerses itself within the landscape. It runs its moist fingers along the surface of the sea, a breathy touch. Couples and their dogs trek the beach leaving trails in the grainy earth.

The ocean is fresh and stale, sweet with abundance and sour with the spoils of human life. There is a little river that ends at a bridge about thirty feet inland. We were told as children not to go in the warm cesspool of pollution. But some ventured in anyway, preferring the warmth of bacteria to the ice of the open ocean.

The water represents so much to me—a place of peace but also a source of fear. Its power and its rumble are felt every night at the house on the cliff, where the walls quake with the impact of ocean on cliff. Once, when I was about five years old, I was playing in the cold March water. I kicked at the foam that was creeping between my toes and shrieked when the cold tongue of seaweed licked my ankles. I was with my aunt and uncle at the time; they were young and weren't paying much attention to me. I waded into the rolling waves, until one powerful rush of ocean swallowed me and dragged me into the retreating water. This was the last time I ever went waist-deep in the ocean. I will never underestimate the power of the water and its gluttonous pull.

Japan felt the full weight of being a tiny land mass in a vast ocean. The earthquake that rocked the city brought along its co-conspirator. The water surged through the city consuming everything it touched. Pieces of that tragedy washed up on the Soquel shore. Their hearts and souls, their fear and suffering melding with the granite sand.

And the part that frightens me most is that it could have so easily been us.

Life is delicate, as precarious as those flowers capping the cliff. We are all broken dolls in the valley of chance, part of Earth's cycle that can be washed away like footprints in the sand.

Our very existence forgotten.

THE INTRUDER

Alexander Papoulias

There's the buzzing again. This time on my upper lip. A sickening sensation that makes me shudder and dry-spit in disgust. I wave my free hand in front of my face, lashing out at the air, and then rub away the microscopic filth from my mouth. That goddamn fly is harassing me. He's doing it on purpose.

That last touchdown was his boldest move yet. The first few were head tickles, then he started exploring the back of my neck. Landing momentarily before I'd writhe to shake him off. Next he discovered my ears. Covered in fine, ultrasensitive hairs that pick up and transmit the faintest change in atmosphere directly to my brain. Mmm. *What treasures are to be found in these caverns?* The buzz would increase suddenly as he zeroed in. But it would disappear the moment I raised my hand off the armrest. He knew what he was doing.

I've been looking forward to this evening. Not a night off exactly, but I take what I can get. Tonight the house is asleep, and I'm alone for a glorious uninterrupted stretch of hours. Just me, my couch, a movie, and a bag of cookies. It's Me time. But I'm not alone.

I had got the laptop just right, perched on a pillow with the power cord in so there'd be no dying battery. Lights out, under a blanket, cookies within reach and ready to disengage. Movie night at Rancho Relaxo. I had barely been through the previews when a faint puff of wind blew against my face. And again. Then he made contact.

His first touches were exploratory. Like being lightly tapped with a piece of electrified cotton, they sent a shiver through my body. Then he grew bold and began to land, longer each time, daring me to swat at my own face, knowing I'd never catch him. All I'd wanted was my Me time, instead I was getting ear-raped by an over inquisitive housefly. Finally, he must have sensed the cookie essence on my lips, and having no fear of my clumsy, sluggish hands, he came in for a taste.

I've heard that every time a fly lands, it defecates. I don't know if that's true, but I know every time I go out to pick up my dog's shit in the yard, it's covered in flies. The same flies I assume, that buzz around my kitchen, land on my food, on my face. When that fuzzy shiver touches my mouth, it's the final insult. The fly dies.

I reach over and click on the lamp, and surprise surprise, the bastard whore is just sitting there on the end-table next to my milk and cookies. Taking a shit, probably. Sitting there, looking up at me, and taking a shit on my goddamned end-table.

My arm goes high in the air. My fist, a hammer ready to nail that fucker straight to hell. I know somehow that I'm making a mistake, but I can't stop it. It's happening faster than my brain can comprehend. Down my fist goes, and the flimsy particle-board end-table implodes and disintegrates. Cool milk rains down on my face, my pillows, and my computer. It pools in the corners of the couch where it mingles with shattered Oreos and turns to a sugary mortar.

Friday, the Lab, trots over and buries her face in a puddle, tail wagging, slurping at the milky crumbs. I get up and go to the kitchen to look for towels and Windex.

Somewhere, a housefly laughs.

Nils, Skin and Tears

Kelly A. Harrison

1989 Bath, England. I'm studying with a group of Americans. We've been away from home for nearly four weeks, and Valentine's day arrives. I hate this holiday, mostly for the social requirements of off-season flowers and poor-quality chocolates. I love this holiday, mostly for the pagan roots, the bacchanalian past.

Nils Petersen, one of our professors, has a tradition of giving a poetry reading to celebrate love and life, so he's determined to recreate some form of this tradition in our new home. We're a rowdy bunch of writers, actors, and (quite oddly) wanna-be policy makers. Quickly, the group has formed a choir, calling themselves the Singing Madrigals. I'm not part of this group because when I sing, dogs in China howl, but I'm enjoying the impromptu singing between classes. Daily, I hear Gilbert and Sullivan duets, fragments mostly, as two people meet in the halls. Annie does a fantastic Ethel Merman to the point I nearly pee my pants when she uses Ethel's voice to restate classroom policies. "You must absolutely, positively, most definitely arrive on time!"

We're gathered now in one of three rooms we've rented for the semester. Nils and the Madrigals sing a song or two, and we're lulled into a state where we're open, receptive, vulnerable. Between songs, Nils reads a poem about first love, the young girl whose shirt lifts when she's at the blackboard and he gets a glimpse of a triangle of flesh. Oh, he says, how one could rise with desire at the sight of such a small sliver of skin.

And then there's Bessie, his first kiss. He compares the knowledge of locker room and playground talk with the reality of kissing a girl who succumbs to his touch, how nothing in the world could prepare him for that, and here, when he's recalling the moment, this man of six feet and six inches, tears up. He's crying over the power of a woman's acceptance of his affections. I've never seen a grown man cry, not like this, not with tears from the world I was taught belonged to women, the world of unfathomable emotions. Men were supposed to be strong, resilient, immune to the swirling emotions that controlled the weaker sex.

And yet I know he is stronger than any other man I've met. I know that his display is genuine, that it makes him more of a man in my eyes, that his response is something that men could have, should have, need to have.

For the first time in my adult life I question our social constructs. Why do we tell men to lock up their feelings? Why am I suddenly discovering that men feel like I feel? Why are men now so suddenly real? I listen to Nils and silently thank him for opening up my world.

Taking Flight

Jessica Keaton

S cooby—dooby—dooo! Scooby dooby doo!"

Me and my cousin are on the front porch playing our favorite game—Scooby Doo. It's where you go forward a few steps and say "Scooby," then back a little bit farther and say "Dooby," then let your feet go into the air as you scream "Doo!"

Joshua's brown hair looks like he put a bowl over his head when he got a haircut. It flops like bunny ears as we go back and forth, back and forth.

The chains sound like they're crying as we go back and forth. I touch them and brown stuff rubs off on my hands. There's a little extra piece of chain that runs halfway down the swing. I shake it and it jingles like loose change.

Nana watches from the yard. Her skin is thin, dark, and splotchy—not like mine. Sometimes, it feels like if I touch her, she'll break. But she doesn't care. She's sitting on one of the sharp rocks around the flower bed weeding the daffodils. They're my favorite. Every time I see them, I want to sniff them and pull them.

Once, I put them in my hair, but then my head started to itch. Turns out there were little, white bugs in the flowers. After that, Nana told me I couldn't pick them anymore, but I think she just didn't want me messing up her flower beds.

"Watch, Nana, watch! Look at us, Nana!"

She looks up and smiles. She wipes her forehead with her arm and smears dirt all over it.

Granddaddy is in another part of the yard on the riding lawnmower. I'm afraid of it because it burned me when I touched what Granddaddy called "the muffler," but I still like to ride on it sometimes. He's wearing the same blue coveralls and orange toboggan he always puts on when he's cutting grass. I wonder if he ever gets tired of wearing the same thing.

We go higher and higher. Almost to the porch ceiling. It feels like we're airplanes flying into the blue sky. We can almost touch the clouds.

The swing starts to slow, so our feet skid on the concrete until it's completely still. We're ready to go again.

"Scooby."

We push forward as far as the chains will take us, almost halfway across the porch. Joshua looks at me, daring me to get scared. But this isn't the Three Little Pigs game and he isn't hiding in the closet as the big bad wolf. I'm ready to fly.

"Dooby."

We push back to the edge of the porch. Our feet are halfway on the concrete and brick and halfway in the air. We're back so far that we're both about to fall out of the swing.

"Doo!"

Our feet are up and we're in the air—it feels like we're going farther than we've even been before. Joshua's feet almost hit the porch light. I look at him and laugh.

But when we go back, it feels different. We're looking at the yard instead of the porch. The wind makes the swing whir as we fly backwards. I see the big magnolia tree that I'm too scared to climb, Nana's prickly pink bushes where we found a snake once, and chopped grass.

Black.

I open my eyes and Joshua can't breathe. It feels like there are rocks on my chest. Nana runs over and I hear the lawnmower turn off. I can't stop laughing. We flew!

Bloody Christmas

Alexander Papoulias

The reasons for not spending the holidays with a writer are many. We are by nature a solitary bunch. Sullen, doubtful, often drunk.

Just as it is a bad idea to rely on a writer to provide sincere, enthusiastic company during the holidays, counting on a writer for anything remotely practical is equal foolishness. If you need a ride home from your Christmas pageant, or someone to hang lights from the eaves of your house and you enlist a writer's help, you can expect to find yourself stranded and your house on fire. A few Christmases ago, my mom was counting on my cooking when we were having about twenty guests over to her house for the big dinner.

I was thankful to have work to do, because being in the kitchen all day would keep me out of mom's crosshairs and give me an excuse to be more or less alone all day. I couldn't be bothered with socializing—I had a bird to roast and carve, a spinach salad with beets and goat cheese, a cornbread stuffing, mashed potatoes, mac and cheese, gravy, biscuits, and pies to make. And there was wine in the kitchen. Thank the little baby Jesus, there was wine.

I'd managed to get the turkey dressed and in the oven when I decided to get the potatoes peeled and sliced. That was going to be the most monotonous and time-consuming job I'd have to face that day, so I poured myself a seventh glass of chardonnay to fortify myself against boredom and I got to it. The brand-new Whustoff chef's knife I'd gotten as an early Christmas present was slicing like a dream and I was just a-chuggin' along, until a slippery-wet potato shot out of my left where I was holding it on the cutting board and razor-sharp German steel came crashing down on my fingers.

There is a moment just after you injure yourself, before the pain arrives, before the heavy bleeding starts, when you are calm and focused and you can take stock of your situation. I used this moment to wrap my mangled hand in a kitchen towel and run out to the garage where I knew there was more wine. I would be spending Christmas day at urgent-care and damned if I was going to do it sober. I drank a bottle of white in double-quick time, and then went inside to inform my brother he'd be driving me to the hospital.

Cooking duties fell to my mother and several guests she enlisted to help her salvage the meal. With no recipes to follow, and harried as she was, mom did not rise to the occasion. I arrived home just in time to eat, with eight stitches and a bottle of Vicodin to ease me gently into the night. I noted, sourly, that the potatoes were full of lumps, the gravy needed salt, the salad was limp and sad. The wine was good though, and I filled my glass with abandon. It was Christmas after all, and I felt like celebrating the season.

Mom was crestfallen about the meal having turned to shit, but I was all warm and cozy and affectionate feeling. I smiled at her with my mouth open and full of turkey and looked around at all the lights and tinsel twinkling and spinning in slow motion as I stuffed my face with my one good hand.

Banker's Hours

Chris Krohn

The house phone in the living room continues to ring. It is ugly, old-school beige plastic, crooning in distress. Who is calling at this hour? Just now, tucked inside my dream was Bob Dylan whispering. Ah, but Woodstock was a hoax, something for the vixens, the vendors, and the capitalist vampires. I struggle to sit up, push my legs out over the side of the aged captain's bed. I hear Dylan again. There was no love fest either, just a bunch of lechers in leotards lampooning a lonely old lioness.

The dachshund-chocolate lab-Chihuahua—my 12-year old daughter calls the San Francisco Retriever--growls as I descend

157

the elegant staircase of this nineteenth century Santa Cruz Victorian. I promptly stumble on the landing, legs not willing to work yet. The rings continue: 11, 12, 13. Is the answering machine full? I wonder.

"Hello, Christopher?" The voice on the other end is female and panting.

"Who's speaking?" I lost my chance meeting with Dylan for this?

"It's Mathilde, your sister-in-law." She is a German war orphan and Pittsburg cosmetics store-owner, married to my older brother for the past ten years.

"What, you okay?" I am unable to say anything more discerning.

"Would I be okay if I was calling you at 3 o'clock in the morning?" Her tone is angry, almost snarky. "The FBI...they were just here. They want your brother."

Her voice surrounds me like an impatient fog. My stomach tightens. I want to go back to bed and hear Dylan. Outside the wind howls pushing the dry spiny fronds of the monkey-puzzle tree closer to the house. My shirt is wet. I impetuously recall a Santa Ana wind scraping at the San Diego coastline many years before.

"I said, show me your badges. They held them up as I cracked open the door." Her voice took on a bemused, almost sinister cadence. "Then I slammed it on 'em, ha!"

Her words roll through my head like bowling pins crashing. "You told them…what?"

"I told them I don't know where my husband is, so get the hell out." I glance down at the hardwood floor and glimpse a puddle of light angling in off a full moon.

"Why is the FBI at your house? What did my brother do?" I am waking up.

"I have no idea what this is about, Christopher, something about a bank. Yes, for God's sake, they are real FBI agents! Two of them are still parked across the street…then after I push the front door shut all of a sudden I hear the garage open and it's my husband. I'm screaming at him like a crazy person, "You gotta get out of here, the FBI is across the street.""

"Was it really the FBI?" I repeat, unable to find anything more pertinent to say.

"Yes, F-B-I." She says this as if talking to a moron. "So he runs into the bedroom, see, throws some clothes in a bag, grabs his gun and starts writing on a fresh sheet of paper."

"Writing?" I suddenly move my body to an upright position. "Writing what?"

"Like his ex-wife's social security number…like I care… his life insurance policy number…mnnnn…his Pittsburgh bank account number. Now those I care about." Her words are quite deliberate, almost whimsical. "Then he starts pacing. Back and forth, back and forth with that gun stuck to his hand like glue." Mathilde pauses. "I hate guns."

"And then what happened?" I can't seem to breathe. Is this really my brother?

"He says, 'They're not getting me, no, not me! I can't do six or seven years in there.'"

"For what?" Now, I am scream.

"All of a sudden, Christopher, he's moving toward the back door. I see him running across the yard, jumping the fence in our backyard. He's gone, just like that. Gone." There is a muffled silence. "Christopher," she shouts without any tears, "what the hell's going on? This doesn't happen to normal people. We're normal people. Oh shit, they are knocking. Gotta go."

An Evening with Kim Addonizio

Sarah Lyn Rogers

The gods are rinsing their just-boiled pasta
in a colander, which is why
it is humid and fitfully raining
down here in the steel sink of mortal life.

"Storm Catechism" by Kim Addonizio

There's no wine back there, is there? Bad move, Alan. I think booze should be obligatory at all of my readings," is Kim Addonizio's opening line when her reading begins at Dr. Martin Luther King Library.

It's ten minutes past seven. The literary crowd that creeps into Center for Literary Arts events is a leisurely one. Many of us are frauds—students attending for extra credit or to fulfill assignments—amidst the genuine fans and faculty. I've just made my way through the glow of nearly-night and the first fat raindrops of the coming downpour to sit beside my friend Katie, who has saved me a spot with a sweatshirt and a smile. I've never read any of Addonizio's poetry, but I figure what the hell, call me a fraud, yes. Empty seats like punched-out teeth fill slowly, quicker now that the poetry reading should already have begun.

When Kim Addonizio approaches the podium, I notice that she is slight—"No bigger than a minute," as my nonni would say—wearing a red and black bustier top and fingerless gloves. A jangle of bracelets brings music to her wrists. She opens with two delicious sonnets, "Stolen Moments" and "So What?" that convince me, along with her outfit, that she is a rock star.

She reads another poem, "Ex-Boyfriends," and I am completely under her spell when the stranger who sat next to me (after the reading had already begun) *quietly answers her cell phone* and carries a conversation about where and when she should be picked up, taking me completely out of the moment. Distractions that would never occur on the page are one drawback to sharing written work in a living, breathing forum—distractions like someone's buttcrack peeping at me from a seat in the front row, and all of the sounds and shifting movements of the local writing community in our stacking seats.

Around the room, I recognize classmates, professors, and other CLA event-goers. I know that I am recognizable to some as a student, but watching Ms. Addonizio devastate the audience with cleverness and a great ear for the musicality of words—while dressed like a punk rock pixie—inspires me. I want someday to be recognizable as a writer, not merely a girl in someone's writing class.

My attention is directed away from the audience as Addonizio reads a story from her forthcoming short story collection, *The Palace of Illusions*, called "Breathe." It's a sweet, sad piece still drawing heavily from the wit and dark humor which colors her poetry. She concludes the evening by playing some blues harmonica, a hobby taken up by "mostly white people now, interestingly." Her breath into the microphone is like a second instrument. Each piece is met with *Yeahs* and *All rights!*

I would like to buy one of Ms. Addonizio's books, but my wallet is at home. My plan is to escape surreptitiously, unrecognizable for now. On our way out, Katie flags Kim Addonizio with a wave and a "Thank you!" before we disappear into the rainy night, no books to sign, no cash on hand. Caught—

in my sense of obligation, and then unprepared in the rain, hair dampening and glasses glistening as I make my way home, mind busy with sonnets and blues harmonica and possibility.

TITLE IN PROGRESS

Amber Stucky

Dear Boyfriend,

I have begun to hate our love with its one hour skin. I have begun to hate our love and its consuming fever. This endless apathy, the eradication of sense that has come along with this relationship. I have begun to hate our love due to its vacant dreams of excitement. Because of this taste of sin, I have died again. I breathed foul and fetid, my heart much too conceited. My mind of shame…are we too mature to play this game? I wonder but only in blind blunder, for I have failed. It was this love that I blackmailed. I licked the stamp the wrong way, painted it the opposite of day. If we could see what should not be, then maybe we could save ourselves from tragedy. I do this often but it's not my obsession. I always wish but it never happens. I can't stand you, you can't stand me. Why are we one when we can't be?

We have tried to leave each other but I wonder…why do we always come back around, fingers outstretched, hearts open like a dartboard, revealing a worn out game.

You were once a cloud floating high in the nebula of my sky, the one that spoke sweet perfection; a scintillating seduction. Our love has deteriorated so badly that I can hear God cackling at this decrepit downfall. As the seasons change, so does my love for you. It is destitute to know that every spring I shall shed you.

You have drained my pain until it became your gain. Our favorite sport has become kicking ourselves in the teeth.

I write this…I write this…but why? There is no clinical term for the damage we are doing nor the damage already done. We are a title in progress. This monotonous circle has burnt itself a rhythm in my soul. I no longer know the way out.

And so the hour starts again…

SNAP!

Maria D'Avolio

It's hard to know exactly if this is the end, because we've been here eight or twelve times, depending on how one counts these things. But maybe I should backtrack. This is a story about the Big Bad Wolf, whom I met shortly after the demise of my twenty-year marriage, and my subsequent attempts to eradicate the beast. I'd lived a sheltered life and had no idea what a wolf looked like, so I fell into his clutches quite unwittingly. OK, maybe there were a few warning signs, like over forty and never married. (My sincere apologies to those who just haven't met the right one, but no absolution for Wolf.) In short, I hadn't even been around the block once and he'd been to Singapore and back. Like ten times. But I didn't find that out until later. He gave me quite the well-rounded education and I think kind of fell for me too, but he preferred the taste of wild game, lots of it. So little Red Riding Hood (me) decided to head back to civilization. It wasn't easy.

Apparently, with the getting over it part, it doesn't matter who ends it, because I've been going through so many mood swings that I realized I needed to take action before my friends, family, and sanity all deserted me. Today I read an article called, "12 Steps to Break Addiction to a Person," and put one of them into action immediately. It's the old rubber-band idea, where you put a rubber-band around your wrist and when you have thoughts you shouldn't, you snap yourself. It started out pretty well, but then I started to think I needed to vary the snaps, depending on the thoughts I was having. Passing thought, like his touch, his scent, one snap. Favorite memories, like him writing me poetry, or hiking at Point Lobos, two snaps. Kissing under my diaphanous leopard scarf while sunbathing at Stinson beach, three snaps. And I think we'll stop there, as you really don't need to hear about my ten-snapper. Within two hours I had a nasty welt on my wrist.

Then I got thinking about the stages to recovering from this thing, from sadness, and thinking of our happy times, to anger, and listening with my fifteen-year-old daughter, Belle, to Taylor Swift songs, like, "I Knew You Were Trouble," "Should Have

Said No," and "We Are Never Getting Back Together." Belle and I belt them out at full volume at every opportunity, because coincidentally, she is going through a similar breakup. We've even thrown in a Pink song, "U + Ur Hand," with Belle doing a rude hand gesture. I didn't reprimand her. Am I a bad mom? Snap. But these songs are also a reminder about how universal this is.

Next phase I think is revenge, which I'm proud to say, I skipped over. Lucky for him that I never ever, even once, thought about pulling a Carrie Underwood on his car. And no, writing about him doesn't count, because I didn't include his name, which has three letters and starts with J, and ends with m, and his last name rhymes with…oops! Have I gone too far?

Last step is recovery. Every once in a while I catch a whiff of it, so can tell a little about it. I've started to do a systematic exorcism of all "our places" so that they no longer contain that pang of heartache and longing when I enter them. For example, I took my friend Chris, who was visiting from the UK, to one of Wolf's and my favorite places in Marin. Chris is happily married with two kids, but while we were ordering he convinced the waitress that he was my ex-husband who came here just to see me and talk me into getting back with him. The waitress was cheering for us to get back together, and the ghosts of the past flew out the door with our laughter. I think I need to take Chris to all our other places.

For now I'm trying to fill the void with lots of exercise, activities with my girls, and taking out my aggressions on the yard with the chainsaw and pickax. I have to admit though that I do miss Wolf's companionship and his fuzzy face. Oops! Snap!

JUST KEEP SWIMMING

Jan McCutcheon

On my fortieth birthday, my husband asked if there was anything I wished I had done, that I hadn't done yet. My reply, "I always wanted to go to Europe," so he booked us a three-week vacation to visit friends in Germany and Spain. When my fiftieth birthday was approaching, and he asked me again, I should have been ready with an answer like, "Visit Paris, France and drink coffee in a café with a view of the Eiffel Tower!" Instead, I foolishly blurted out, "I've always been sorry I never learned to swim!"

And so it began. My husband and daughter took me every day for three weeks to a friend's swimming pool, where they proceeded to instruct, advise, bully, threaten, and terrorize me, in an effort to teach me to swim. I tried, I cried, and I complained bitterly the entire time. I mentioned every day how I hated swimming, how the water got into my sinuses and my ears, how I was sure I had some sort of lung problem due to swallowing copious amounts of chlorine. Overall, I was a giant pain in the ass.

They didn't let my lack of cooperation deter them. They decided they would teach me to swim or kill me trying. It was unclear which result they would achieve. Every afternoon, the three of us would drive to the pool while I would sulk and they would give me swimming advice. Some of the advice given: "Just BREATHE when you turn your head, and DON'T BREATHE when your face is in the water!" and "If you get really scared, JUST STAND UP, the water is only four feet deep!" These pointers might sound helpful, but I just couldn't seem to get the hang of it.

On the last day of the third week, they determined that I could swim well enough to join the YMCA where I could continue to practice. We repeated our familiar ritual every weekend, with me sulking and complaining while they continued to give me encouragement. My daughter's encouragement went something like: "I can see you freaking out under the water! Just stand up!"

She referred to my style as "swim-walking." My husband kept telling me that I would eventually feel the water supporting me, but I kept saying that the water was not supporting me; it was trying to kill me.

After nearly a year of weekend practice, we were driving home from the pool, and I wasn't complaining. I was thinking about what had just happened and blurted out, "Oh my God, I love swimming!" Now I can feel the clear water supporting me and gently flowing over my skin. The blue color of the pool is calming. And instead of the sound of my thrashing around in panic—and my family yelling at me—now I hear nothing but the sound of bubbles.

THE TEST

Ria Vyas

My head was pounding, my vision blinded by my tear-filled eyes. And I tried to breathe but there was no air. I wanted to move, speak, run away, do something, but I could not move; the room, my mother, everything was spinning around me in a frenzy, except me. I felt stuck. I wanted to scream, vocalize how I felt, but instead, I just stood there, frozen. I was in my own little world with a million different thoughts running through my head but I could not focus on a single one of them for longer than a split second. It was the most horrible and painful feeling in the world. I felt like

I was sinking into a dark black hole and the harder I struggled to breathe, the deeper I sunk. I was fourteen years old and as far away from normal as I could possibly be. This moment was the very beginning of my journey I now call, The Test.

A month earlier I had moved to India with my mother so that we could try to settle down before my school year began. My father had explained that he had some unfinished business and that he would join us as soon as he could. However, I knew there were issues that had not been fully explained to me. My parents' constant worried expressions and steady fighting combined with the police showing up with a warrant and searching our house before our sudden and mysterious move across the seven seas were enough to give away that our situation was far from happy or perfect. As expected, even though we were staying with my grandparents I was unhappy all the time and to make matters worse my father was constantly calling to tell us he was going to be in California "Just a little while longer." I just couldn't understand why everyone was acting like everything was fine when any idiot could see that nothing was normal or fine at all.

One night, the phone rang in the middle of my peaceful slumber. Its shrill tone threw me out of my dream and immediately woke me up. I heard my mother answer it but I kept listening. The conversation was soft and I heard the door quickly shut. I felt like I was in a movie and this was my climax. I leaped out of my bed and threw my mother's door open. My aunt, my mom, and my grandparents were all in tears and no one could look at me.

"What did Dad do?" I whispered. Deep down, I already knew he had done something horrific and despite having a premonition, I had to hear it out loud. It was like hearing the dreadful words from my beautiful mother's mouth would made this shocking and even sickening nightmare a harsh reality to me. Finally, my mother's weak and broken voice shattered the silence. She pulled me close to her and said, "Your father has made some horrible mistakes and has done some terrible things and he has been arrested for tax evasion and fraud. He will remain in prison until the trial is over. I was stunned, shocked, and petrified. At that exact moment, my life as I knew it was officially over.

I stood in front of my mother, head spinning and frozen, with tears rolling down my face and as she stared back into my devastated eyes, somehow she found her strength. She grasped my hands tightly in hers and said, "I love you more than anything in this world and we will get through this. We're a team and we will find a way to survive this. I promise you, we will pass this Test."

So, we made a promise to each other to "just keep swimming," and as a team, my mother and I passed our Test. No matter how dark or gloomy our road became, we did not succumb and we did not rescind. Instead, we learned our fate is up to us, and us alone.

PLUS OR MINUS

Emily Wood

S even days late. I checked every hour and still there was no dark red stain in my panties. It was junior year of high school, soon it would be summer and I would be free. I would be free, if I wasn't pregnant.

I arrived at school and my boyfriend, Brian, handed me the pregnancy test. We met at our usual meeting spot, in the woods behind the school.

"Do you really think you're…" he said with a look of *holy fuck* on his face.

"I'm seven days late and I am usually never late."

He nodded silently. He didn't actually want to know. I think most men are always perplexed by the happenings down there. They must think magical, mysterious things happen *down there*.

I waited four excruciating hours until lunch, then me and my best friends Libby and Kristen went to the second floor women's restroom and locked it. We could hear Brian and his friends gathered outside. I picked a stall and went in holding the two sticks while Libby and Kristen stood outside.

"Step one, remove test from packaging," Libby read in a serious tone.

"They have pictures," Kristen said as she laughed her usual girlish giggle.

"Libs!" I shouted from the stall.

"Step two, pee on applicator. Then shake and wait fifteen minutes. A pink plus means pregnant, and a blue minus means not pregnant."

I peed on both tests; I wanted to be doubly sure.

"I think this is the only test I want to fail."

I pulled up my jeans and left the stall. I set the two tests on the sink and waited. The longest fifteen minutes of my life. None of us spoke, we were all unsure of what to say. Libby braided my hair and Kristen listened to music and redid her makeup. Some girls began to knock on the door.

"Open up. This is a public restroom. You can't lock the door. Or is it so you little whores can take your pregnancy tests." I started crying. I could hear Brian telling her to use another bathroom that that was his girlfriend and to shut the fuck up.

Our friend Skyla had had a scare a couple of months ago and we went through this routine then too.

"Katie has no right...." Libby's eyes burned a hole through the door.

The timer went off. We checked the applicators. Two pink plusses.

"Shit, I'm sorry." They said at the same time, and turned to hug me.

"One of you go tell Brian but I can't do this right now," I said through tears. My hand flew to my stomach, like I had seen on so many made for TV movies. "I'm pregnant."

CHRISTMAS IN IMAGES

Jessica Keaton

The wooden church with the green roof sits in the cotton snow underneath the Christmas tree. A sole light bulb illuminates it from the inside out—like every year. Above it, the pine needles are making the air smell like the pine tree hanging from the rearview mirror of Daddy's car. It's not Christmas without that smell.

I'm playing with my Little Tyke's Noah's Ark set. You can tell it's that brand because all of the figurines are short and plump. First, the yellow lion goes into the boat, then the gray elephant, then the white polar bear. Each time I drop one of them onto the boat, the sound of plastic hitting plastic blends in with the voices in the kitchen behind me.

Cousins, cousins, and more cousins. That's the only time I see all of them in one place. Robin, my oldest cousin, has dark hair—like me—and is holding a plastic cup and smiling. Next to her, Chris, the next oldest, stands with one hand on the counter. He has short hair and works at Baskin-Robbins. Sometimes, he gives me free ice cream. Lindsay is the next. She has the most beautiful blonde hair and she clogs with me. I hope that I'm as good as she is one day. The youngest cousin is Joshua. I see him every day. He comes over and we play together, but he usually finds a way to scare me and make me cry.

Aunt Linda and Nana are somewhere, shuffling around. I'm not sure exactly where they are, but I can hear their shrill voices. Neither of them will sit down until the food is ready—Nana with her short, dark curls and Aunt Linda with her pale, thin hair.

Nana isn't really a good cook. The only good things she can make are deviled eggs. They look like Christmas—red from paprika. The halves are placed on a red tray and passed around to the cousins and me.

Daddy is the only one who will tell Nana she's a bad cook. He's the only one that, deep down, isn't afraid of her. When she's mad, she's scary. Her face will turn reddish purple, like a plumb. I've only seen her mad at Granddaddy and Daddy. I don't think she's ever been mad at me.

Where is Daddy? Where is Granddaddy? I'm not sure where Daddy is, but Granddaddy is snoring in his recliner by the gas heater across from me—the blue flames reaching toward the ceiling. Every so often, he'll stop snoring and it will sound like he's not breathing. Then, he'll make one loud sound and start snoring again.

"Hyatt? Hyatt! Wake up!" Nana will scream.

"Huh? What? I'm awake," he'll say, then doze off again.

Nana will roll her eyes and go back to the kitchen to check on the chicken and rice. It tastes like mush. It needs lots of salt.

Somewhere, there's apple cider being poured into plastic cups. It blends perfectly with the smell of the tree. Nana has changed the tablecloth to the red, plastic one with the poinsettias. They're supposed to signify something about Jesus, but I can't remember the story.

The cousins' voices sound like the whirring of the refrigerator—blending together to make the perfect backdrop of Noah's flood. I load the rest of my people—Noah, his wife, and a couple of odd policemen—and lift the boat into the air.

It rocks and sways, looking almost like it's enjoying itself. Like it's praying for the flood to last.

Lunch Break

Brett Vickers

There was a paved fire road that winded its way through Mesa Verde Middle School in San Diego, California. It was lunch time, and the six of us were sitting on the curb in the center of campus, leaning over the food propped on our laps. Out of the entire group, I was only friends with Kevin—and even that friendship was slipping. We used to be good friends. Great friends even. Best friends.

But things changed, as they are prone to do.

Our sisters were on the same travel softball team, but the intricate nature of sports politics had recently alienated our parents. We never saw each other outside of school anymore. Our parents wanted nothing to do with each other.

Kevin crumpled his brown bag into a small ball and rolled it into the gutter. He turned over onto his stomach and grabbed the lip of the curb with his hands while his feet remained on the street. It looked like he was doing pushups on the ground, the way he lowered his body and raised it with the bend of the elbows.

He groaned. "God, I want to bang two girls at once." He kept thrusting his pelvis toward the ground. Everyone laughed.

The talk turned to the girls at our school—as it often did in this group. Who'd they want to have sex with, who would be willing, who already lost their virginity—these were the bullet points of their conversations that were always being recycled. I was a late bloomer maybe, I didn't see the point of talking about girls that way. It was strange hearing Kevin participate in the talk. I didn't like it. He used to be like me, avoiding the spotlight, being a listener and not a speaker, never one to offend. Now he was the initiator.

I was feeling nervous about what they were talking about. I didn't want to look at what they were doing with their fingers, their tongues. I didn't want the curb I was sitting on to be a prop for their fantasy. I wanted to walk away. None of it felt like something people should talk about. I kept my head down and focused on my sandwich, my chips, my shoes until the bell rang and swept away their words and gestures.

Their sudden silence was heavy. It curled around my back, pushed down on my spine, and forced my head up.

They were all looking at me.

Me.

The outsider. The non-contributor. The unknown. The potential tattler.

I looked back down.

"Brett won't tell," Kevin said. "He's cool."

I met Kevin's eyes. They were pleading with me, begging me to make his declaration true. Don't tell, they said. Be cool.

I remained silent, I didn't understand what they wanted from me, what Kevin wanted from me, or why he was trying to include me in on a secret I wanted no part of. Their attention was suffocating. It felt like they were pouring their filth into my soul and washing their hands clean, using my conscience as a washcloth.

"You won't tell, will you, Brett?" Kevin asked, his tone became desperate. "You won't tell anyone what we were talking about, right?"

What would I say? And to whom? What answer did they even want to hear from me? Looking back, I suspect that they wanted to hear confirmation that their conversation would be kept secret, that I wouldn't share with anyone—especially not an authoritative figure like a teacher—what the nature of their topic was. But why would I do that? And, even worse, why would they think I would?

All I could muster was a slow, sad shake of the head. No, I wouldn't tell.

They nodded their heads at me, knowing I was telling the truth, letting me know that they never doubted me for a moment. Kevin was smiling, but he looked sad. He looked caught. He looked lost.

And after that lunch period, I never found him again.

THREE HOURS

Emily Wood

I stare at my digital clock's red flashing numbers, as the alarm goes off. It reads 5:00AM. In two hours I will be in the testing center, taking my African literature final. My boyfriend, Kevin, snores beside me. The asshole stole two hours of sleep, so that I only got three hours of crappy sleep.

We went to bed at midnight. I had been wired on Red Bull for hours, busy cranking out the last of my notebook for my writing fiction class, and cramming for tomorrow's 7:00AM test. As soon as Kevin's head hit the pillow, he was asleep and snoring. I turn to him. Lucky bastard, sleep came so easily for him. I am too stressed; sleep doesn't come. After twenty minutes of staring at the clock desperately waiting for sleep, as my brain finally starts to drift off into sleep deprived unconsciousness, Kevin turns so his mouth is half an inch from my face. He lets out a loud snore and exhales hot air on my ear. My eyes flutter open. I give him a gentle kick. "Kevin stop snoring." He grunts and rolls over. Minutes of sleep come. A sleep that is void of dreams, instead a flickering of thoughts pass by.

I am woken again by Kevin's droning snores. I stare at the clock once more. That was twenty minutes of uninterrupted sleep. I turn over, face Kevin, and pin him down. "If you don't stop snoring, I will punch you in the fucking face," I say snarling. He doesn't even open his eyes; he just rolls over.

As half unconscious thoughts pass by, I grip my pillow and visualize. Smothering him. His snores stop, he lets out a whimper, and his legs kick out one final time. I lift the pillow and see his still face. Finally some peace and quiet!

I turn from the clock's numbers to his still sleeping body. I guess I didn't kill him after all. I shake him vigorously. "You stole two hours asshole! Now wake up and feel my pain. You are going to quiz me for my test and drive me in." His eyes pop open.

Yep, definitely still alive.

THINGS SHARED

Jesse Mardian

I have this friend, let's just call him Marcus. So Marcus had just returned from a semester abroad. While away, he had told me everything. There were emails, postcards, letters. Sometimes he called from a payphone. He had had himself quite a time. So, when he returned I knew he was in trouble.

He had told her everything too, except the part about the girl, of course. I don't know how she later found out, probably from the Internet. Everything can be found out on the Internet.

Anyways, when Marcus got back he told her he wasn't feeling well. It was a touchy subject. He lied about the details. He went to the doctor. The doctor ran a test. And he was told that the results would come back in a week or two. During this time he was half himself. You could see it in his eyes—always looking at something not there. He drank more, and it affected him. He told me about going soft. For the two weeks he was a slave for the result.

One night we were drinking together on my porch. I was glad to have him back. Just like the old times. Just like he'd never left. At first, he acted like he used to, being sarcastic, crass, but funny. He used to see the world as a joke. But things change. Between sips, he would stare off into the street, probably remembering. Finally, when it was quiet, he told me, "I've never felt so much self-loathing in my life."

I remember the email he had sent me. He wrote that he had done it against a church door. Or at least he thought it was a church door. Those fallen oranges that the city is famous for were scattered along the gutters. People were passing as they were going at it. He wrote that the sun rose as he finished. He wrote that it was the first time. But of the girl, he wrote little.

"The other night Linda touched me," he said with a weak voice, "and I had to move her hand away. How am I supposed to tell her of things that will break her?"

He cried. It was real. If I wasn't such a lousy friend I would have said something meaningful. But when you are young, you are selfish.

"Just forget about it," I said, "She'll never know."

A week later he got the call. He learned he was clean. But by then the damage had already been done. She knew something was wrong. A rift had been made. And it pains me to know that if he had just come back without a conscience everything would have turned out just fine.

After his girlfriend left him, Marcus moved in with me. It's hard to watch a friend crumble. Pathetic, really. But I thought I could help him get back on his feet. I took him out, bought him drinks, and tried to revive him, yet he wasn't ready.

"The world's a joke, right?" I said to him one night at the pub.

Marcus sat there staring at his whiskey glass, half-empty.

"Yeah, a real fucking joke."

That night, driving home, Marcus passed out in the passenger seat. Seeing him like that, cradled like an infant with his head against the window, put things into perspective. We all make mistakes. We are all fucked up. But he is lucky enough to still be young. So much ahead. As Marcus lay there, I thought of these things and I couldn't wait to tell him.

Rushing

Steve "Spike" Wong

It was 1973 and I should have lost my finger. High up on one of Yosemite's granite walls, my entire body was dangling by one finger held in the wire loop of a piece of climbing gear, and that piece was fixed into a granite crack by the stubborn force of friction. My feet had slipped while I was placing the gear, and as my 155 body pounds plus twenty-five gear pounds flew off the rock, my right forefinger found the wire loop of a climbing nut that I had just placed. I screamed with a combination of pain, anger, fear, and survival instinct. My bulging eyes willed my finger to stay in one piece and every last drop of strength concentrated into my right forearm and hand. My partner, Tim, must have been impressed. Down below on a ledge, at the other end of the rope, he was screaming, "Stick it!" And in fact I did. My feet came up from their dangling, pasted themselves onto the blank rock, and just as I was weighting them, the nut broke loose and I flipped backwards. Seventy feet later I hit the end of the rope. I was hanging in space about thirty feet away from and level with Tim, who was securely belaying me. He was staring, wide-eyed, as if he had half expected me to continue falling to my untimely death. Little did we know that he was rushing toward his.

Climbing is an equipment intensive sport like no other. Every piece of gear is important for one reason: neglect a single piece, no matter how small, and it could cause one's death. Even free soloists, who generally carry no gear and use no ropes, are reliant on their climbing shoes, and lack of attention to them will surely kill. Because of this attention to equipment, certain pieces become favorites, coddled and cared for like a new mistress. These days, I have been known, for example, to sleep with my ice axes inside the tent, rather than leave them totally alone outside. They are a matched set of carbon fiber tools, very expensive, and yet dear to me far beyond the monetary value. I have also been known to buy new climbing ropes at the drop of a pebble, because the last thing I want to worry about is whether or not a rope is, shall we say, becoming suspect. I do not even want to entertain the thought.

The nut that blew out of the rock, and which I still had my finger wrapped around when I hit the end of the rope, was purchased in Yosemite Valley in 1971, the year I started climbing with Tim. It was his piece, identified with his trademark red tape. But as I floated roughly at the end of the rope, I could hardly tell the tape from the blood. There was a lot of red oozing from a grated spot on my wrist and a tear in my finger. Tim stared and asked, "What the hell?"

I hurt like hell, too, but the first thing I did was to clip that nut to the gear sling. I didn't want to drop it because I knew how poor we were, and yet in our poverty we had done everything possible to buy good climbing gear. There is no use in equipping oneself with cheap climbing tools; it is almost oxymoronic to suggest such a thing. And it would insult our friendship if I didn't care for Tim's gear the way I cared for mine; our meager pile of equipment was nearly sacred to us. It would, in fact, serve us flawlessly as we topped out on the climb the next day.

The next summer, Tim was attempting to climb a new route in the High Sierra. Halfway up a beautiful rock wall, he slipped. The force of his fall pulled his gear out of the rock. He impacted a ledge and died from internal injuries as his partner was running twenty miles out to summon a rescue helicopter.

Tim's widow gave me all of his gear, every last piece. When I had the heart to, I sorted through it all and found the one wired nut that had almost torn my finger off. Everything else I gave away; the memories were too painful. That one piece rests in my car, reminding me of my best friend. It prods me daily to remember that I, too, may be rushing toward the unknown.

Visual art by Emily Wood

ABOUT THE AUTHORS

Adnan Adnan is originally from Jessore, Bangladesh. He was born in 1979. He moved to the United States in 1997, and now lives in San José, California. He is an electrical engineer, and creative nonfiction MFA candidate at San José State University. In 2001, he published a book of poetry in Bengali, and in 2008 won a Peace Poetry Contest from the Santa Clara County. He is currently working on his memoir, The Family Fables. Adnan Adnan's works have appeared on the Flash Fiction World, Mukto-Mona, and The Rumpus. In 2013, he won the Ruth MacLean McGee Award for Outstanding Achievement in Non-Fiction.

Jesse Buchanan is a strange man, often looked at with a combination of awe and horror. Having attained his Associate Arts from Foothill College in 2013, he is working his way toward his Bachelors in English at San José State University, and well on the path toward his goals. His continued education is his primary goal with a future desire to write short stories, novels, and creative interactive works, such as Role Playing Games and read-as-you-play game books.

Valerie Cruz is going to school for her Master's in English at San José State University, and plans to complete her degree in the spring of 2014. She is originally from Tulare, California, and received her Bachelor's in Literature from UC Merced. This submission was initially written for a memoir class and was Valerie's first experience in writing creative nonfiction. She plans to explore further into this field in her writing.

Sage Curtis graduated from San José State University as a double major in Creative Writing and Journalism. Primarily a poet, Sage has also attended writing programs at UC Berkeley and CSU Monterey and plans to pursue her MFA in the coming year. In 2013, she received the Dorrit Sibley Award for Outstanding Achievement in Writing and Studying Poetry and a California College Media Award for Feature Writing. She has also had a poem published in "Brilliant: A Student Anthology." While at SJSU, she worked as a reporter, features editor, and production editor at the Spartan Daily and studied abroad in Germany. Her poetry can be viewed through her personal blog: thewordsofsagedanielle.blogspot.com.

Maria D'Avolio comes from a large, boisterous, and really fun Italian family, about whom she has written extensively. She also has two teenage daughters who provide much rich fodder for essays, but sadly are a bit reticent about appearing in print. Maria has had to make due with more tame material, and is currently working on a book of essays, with names changed to protect the innocent. A recent transplant to the Los Gatos mountains, she is also a chai addict, and eats copious amounts of dark chocolate to inspire her writing.

Shannon Daly is a 20-something San José State University alumnus who loves to read, write, and fish—but not at the same time. She works as a technical writer for a data integration software company in the Bay Area.

Ashley Florimonte is a poet and short story writer of both fiction and nonfiction. She graduated with a degree in English from San José State University and spends her free time writing, stretching, and laughing uncontrollably.

Kelly A. Harrison is a writer living in San José, CA. She's currently working on *The Body Remembered*, a novel about body memory, sexual abuse, and their effects on the birth experience. After spending years in the high-tech industry, Kelly changed careers and is now teaching at San José State University.

Jessica Keaton is a cat person who is currently pursuing her MFA in Creative Nonfiction at San José State University. Originally from Georgia, the land of humidity and Baptists, she has converted to the California lifestyle without forgetting her life-changing sweet tea recipe.

Chris Krohn is, as he calls it, a "NewYorkinCal Writer" who has been practicing literary journalism since his teens. After teaching and writing stints in Sandinista Nicaragua and Oscar Arias' peaceship Costa Rica in the late 1980's, he returned to California to study society's landfill 'use and reuse' patterns. As a result, he won a seat on the Santa Cruz City Council, eventually becoming Mayor. Since writing profiles of activists at the Democratic National Convention in Boston in 2004 for the Berkeley Daily Planet, he has been hooked on the creative nonfiction genre. Although he lives in Santa Cruz, his California dreams always have him moving in and around his New York past.

Jon Linsao is an English student at San José State University. He has authored multiple short stories, memoirs, and essays, but "A Conversation with Myself" is the first piece he has submitted for publication. He is currently working on his first novel and hopes to finish before the year's end.

Deena Majeed is a Palestinian-American who lives in California. She loves reading, driving down the beautiful California coast, and her baby daughter. Her favorite authors are Khaled Hosseini, Gabriel Garcia Marquez, and John Steinbeck.

Jesse Mardian is an MFA student. Jesse is a substitute teacher. Jesse is poor. Jesse drinks. Jesse writes.

Cathleen Miller is a nonfiction writer based in the San Francisco Bay Area. Her latest work is *Champion of Choice*, the biography of UN leader Nafis Sadik. Miller's previous work includes *Desert Flower*, the story of activist Waris Dirie which describes the Somali nomad's experience with female genital mutilation; this memoir was later adapted as a feature film and released in 34 nations. The print version has become an international sensation, selling 11 million copies in 55 languages and has played a major role in outlawing genital mutilation. In both *Desert Flower* and *Champion of Choice* Miller utilizes her signature strategy: the application of storytelling to demonstrate how the issues which affect one individual are representative of a larger world order. The personal is political.

Marcus Moonshoe was never born. His very essence permeated the air and fell into a vessel here on Earth. The vessel was a young boy. The spirit was Plutonian. Through the years he began to acclimate to the human way of life and actually fit in quite well.

Onette Morales graduated from San José State University in the spring of 2013. She is currently pursuing her single-subject teaching credential at San José State University. She hopes to become a high school English teacher in the next few years. Aside from reading and writing, Onette enjoys hiking, dancing, and wine tasting in her spare time.

Amanda Morin is a California native who loves to write about beautiful places and beautiful people. She is currently pursuing her MFA at San José State University.

Nahida S. Nisa is a mermaid.

Alexander Papoulias is a writer and bookseller from Sunnyvale, California. He is currently at work on a book about one or more human beings who are involved in a situation. The details of which remain unresolved at this time.

Tara Phillips graduated from San José State University in May with a BA in English and Creative Writing. She earned a Catherine Urban Scholarship in 2012 and the Lois King Thore Short Story

Award in 2013. Tara works part-time as a Radiologic Technologist and sings for fun. She is currently working on a collection of short stories and preparing other work for publication.

Sarah Lyn Rogers is a poet, author, and illustrator pursuing her MFA in Creative Writing at San José State University. In Spring 2013, she received the James Phelan Literary Awards in Metrical Verse under Thirty Lines, Free Verse over Thirty Lines, and first place in Familiar Essay. Two of her poems, "Spider Hands," and "Familiar," were selected for publication in Issue #31 of *Chantarelle's Notebook*. When she isn't reading or writing, Sarah provides percussion, backing vocals, and hand painted album artwork for Elflock, an ethereal alternative rock band based in the South Bay.

Marc Solkov is a writer and procrastinator.

Amber Stucky is an aficionado on agony and atrocity; a misogynistic mammal ruined by mayhem; a brilliant brat burdened by blame; an eager existence drugged on ennui; a raconteur bent on revenge.

Manni Valencia is a brilliant drunken workout beast and a badass writer. He looks to authors Neil Gaiman and Brian K. Vaughan for inspiration and unspoken rivalry. Manni is currently working on the story of his life.

Brett Vickers says, "There are only two things that Brett Vickers hates: people that talk in the third-person and people that talk about themselves."

Jennifer Voight graduated Magna Cum Laude from San José State University where she discovered and continues to celebrate the bond which unites syntax and elegance in the English language. She lives with her husband and too many pets in Almaden, California and commits herself daily to the comforts of a geriatric golden retriever named Biskit and to writing her bad-ass self into history.

Ria Vyas was born and raised in Mountain View, California and has resided in the Bay Area for most of her life. At the age of fourteen, her family moved to India for four years and after high school, she returned to her home town in California unaccompanied by any other family members, ready to build her life as an adult and be fully responsible for herself. She recently graduated from San José State with a Bachelor of Arts degree in English and with a minor in Kinesiology and is now pursuing her teaching credential at San José State University. Ria has always had passion for writing and this is her first piece of hopefully many published works.

Emily Wood's six word bio: blind girl mostly alone never scared.

Candice Wynne spent decades through the gauntlet of her life when one day she decided it was time to step across the threshold of conventionality to discover the world one country, one train ride, one curious footstep at a time. She holds an MFA in Narrative Nonfiction at San José State University.

ACKNOWLEDGMENTS

Spike acknowledges that a boatload of free and powerful spirits have contributed to his well-being and creativity. Among these are: his parents Ernie and Alice, for supporting his early flights of imagination, his wife Debbie Zehnder, for inciting courage and belief, his kids Devin and Margo for adding their own zest and humor to his life, and Wilma Marcus-Chandler, for unfailingly believing in his humanity and soul. And to the rest of the boatload, Spike remembers you all and he is mightily grateful for all of your acceptance, understanding, and shared tomfoolery.

Jan would like to thank her family: her father Harry McCutcheon for encouraging her from an early age to read,

read, read, her husband Jaime De los Ríos for paying the bills during this project, Nick Kukich for saying he's proud of his mom, and Fiona De los Ríos-McCutcheon for facilitating the editor meetings, including the occasional eye-roll when needed. Jan would also like to thank Nick Flynn and Cheryl Strayed for inspiration, Scott Lankford for early encouragement, Ben the Barista for supplying the necessary caffeine, and Kelly Harrison for applying her expertise in proofreading. And, of course, she would like to thank Harry the Dog for his loyal companionship throughout.

AFTERWORD

Three.

Please participate.
Email THREEasin3@gmail.com for submission guidelines.